15742

D0116830

Ten Great
Basketball Offenses

Ten Great Basketball Offenses

Dr. William A. Healey
and
Joseph W. Hartley

Parker Publishing Company, Inc.
West Nyack, N. Y.

PRINTED IN THE UNITED STATES OF AMERICA
ISBN—0-13-903294-0
BC

Dedication

To two girls . . .
for Bill—it is Ruth,
for Joe—it is Beryl.

Why We Wrote This Book
and What It Will Do for You

Today in basketball there are almost as many offenses in use as there are coaches. Each coach has his own offense, and of course it varies and differs from year to year to fit and adjust to the talent at hand. Yet in spite of this, many offenses are similar, and in most instances are patterned after one of the "Great Offenses" that has been used by a great team or a great coach who devised a "system" or an "offense" that has been in use for a period of time and has proven successful.

The problem of selecting the proper offense for the material at hand is an age-old coaching problem, both for the experienced and young beginning coach. Most coaches in beginning their career select a basic type pattern or style of play, usually determined by the experiences they have had and the coaches they have played under and been associated with. As their career develops they become more individualistic and develop their own ideas, depending on the material they have, and the existing conditions under which they coach. Development of the game and changes in the rules also affect the development of offenses and styles developed by coaches.

To our knowledge no book has ever been written which has been devoted entirely to the "Great Offenses" that have been used and have proven to be successful. For this reason the authors have decided to give the basics of at least "Ten Great Offenses," or what we believe to be the "Ten Greatest Offenses." In giving the basics of these offenses, we also will give some detail and options to each, and enough information that any coach could take the offense and from the basics given, adapt the

offense to fit his needs in a given situation. For this reason we believe this
book will be valuable to all coaches and students of the game of basketball.

Another purpose the authors have in mind in presenting this book
is to give the basketball coaching profession a book that presents in one
compact package at least "Ten Great Basketball Offenses" in such a form
as to be helpful should a coach want to know more details of one of these
offenses that is commonly in use. It is also hoped that this book will be a
help to other coaches in developing their own offenses which may be a
variation of, or a combination of, some of the "Great Basketball Offenses."

BILL HEALEY AND JOE HARTLEY

Table of Contents

9

Transition from defense to offense in the fast break. Fast break opportunities. Parts of the fast break. Keys to a successful fast break. Types of fast breaks. Basic patterns.

Offenses against the 1-3-1, 2-2-1, 2-1-2, and other zone defenses. Offensive theories for use against the zone. Basic principles of breaking the zone defense. Continuity of play to beat the zone. Basic plays and patterns.

Key to the Diagrams

O   Offensive Player

X   Defensive Player

⟶   Path of Player

◌   Offensive Player Breaks to Here

X̣   Defensive Player Breaks to Here

●   Ball Starts Here

- - -⟶   Path of Pass

· · · · ·▷   Shot or Rebound

⟞   Screen or Rebound Position

∿⟶   Dribble

⌢⟶   Pivot or Roll

—| | | | |⟶   Staccato Steps

Ten Great
Basketball Offenses

1

The Single
Pivot-Post Offense

The most universally used offense in the game of basketball through-out its history has been the Single Pivot-Post offense, or some variation of it. For a period of time during the development of the game, so universal was the use of this offense that there may have been doubts about the existence of any other type of offense. Even today with the development of many offensive innovations, styles, and patterns, the Single Pivot-Post offense is still used by more teams than any other offense. Thus it is that the authors feel that this book should begin with the Single Pivot-Post offense. So many teams have become famous using this offense that they are too numerous to mention, and it would be unfair to mention only a few.

Many stories are told about the origin of the Pivot-Post offense. The most celebrated story is the one told about its origin with the New York Celtics. This version says it was early in the basketball season of 1924 and the Celtics were playing in Rochester, New York. Dutch Dehnert was overweight and not conditioned to the pace of the weaving Celtic offense. After a time he became so tired that he moved down court and stationed himself in an area near the foul line with his back to the basket. Nat Holman flipped the ball to Dutch and Johnny Beckman cut over the top and in front of Dehnert so close that he bumped his tight defensive man into him. Beckman was in the clear and Dutch threw him the ball for an easy layup shot. This story says that at that moment the Pivot-Post offense was born.

Another version centering around the Celtics comes from Cy Miller, a former player on a team called the Tennessee Rail Lites (the Rail Lites were famous in themselves, and often toured with the Celtics), and Cy in giving a similar version to the one just mentioned, says it all happened in Chattanooga.

No doubt the people of Kentucky think that Adolph Rupp invented it. Then there is the story told down in Missouri, that the offense originated one night in, of all places, the small town of Lathrop. From a game being played there one night in the 1920's comes the story that the gym was small and that there was a concrete pillar in the middle of the floor. Quite by accident one player dribbled around this post and lost his defensive man as he bumped into the post. He continued to use the post for this purpose very effectively the rest of the game. In thinking this situation over after the game and wondering how he would lose this defensive man when they were to play a return match with no post obstruction on the floor, he struck upon the idea of stationing the largest and least mobile teammate on a spot near the foul line and with his back to the basket. This was done, and with so much effectiveness that here the Pivot-Post play was born, so this story goes. Soon the idea developed of passing the ball to the post man with teammates cutting by him for a return pass. Too, very soon, the more agile pivot-post men began to fake passes, turn and maneuver for shots off the play themselves.

Long before either of these commonly told stories fell upon familiar ears, many other stories had been told about the origin of the Pivot-Post offense. Probably each community, state, or region has similar stories about the origin of this play, and this offense. Regardless, in 1925 the original New York Celtics had developed the offense into a very effective scoring weapon, and as they traveled throughout the country, the idea caught on rapidly. Soon the offense was being used everywhere. It became so commonly used, that one can't help but wonder what basketball offenses must have been like from 1891 until 1925.

The Pivot-Post play and the offense has had a profound affect upon rule changes that have been made in the game. In the early days of the game, tall players and big players were not as plentiful as they are today. In fact, in those days a 6'3" player was a prize, and lucky was the team that had one such player. Always the tallest and most robust player was used as the Pivot-Post player. Competition became keen to secure taller and bigger players. As they increased in stature, they were stationed nearer the basket, and finally right in front of it. Play in front of the basket became rough as physical contact developed resulting from the defensive player's efforts to dislodge the Pivot-Post players out of their favored scoring positions in front of the basket. Something had to be done about this rough play, and in 1932 the rules makers passed the three-second lane rule. The rule was passed with the idea of not allowing the big Pivot-Post player to station himself right in front of the basket with the thought that this would eliminate much of the rough play around the basket area. At that time the free throw lane was only six feet wide. In 1955 the free throw lane was widened to 12 feet for college and A.A.U. courts and in 1957 the rule was applied to all courts as a further effort to legislate on the developments that came from the Pivot-Post play.

Today the International Rules have further widened the lane, and there is always the possibility that our National Alliance Rules Committee might someday adopt this widened free throw lane area as it is now played under the International Rules in Olympic Competition. While it is possible that such rules legislation can change the style and type of play around the basket area, it is doubtful that the Pivot-Post offense can ever be entirely eliminated. There will always be some fragments of the offense left, regardless of rule legislation.

ADVANTAGES OF THE SINGLE PIVOT-POST OFFENSE

The Single Pivot-Post offense has many advantages and these advantages no doubt account for its popularity and wide use since the origin of the offense. Here are some advantages that can be given:

1. In most situations the talent of the players available can best be adapted and used in some phase of this offense.
2. The offense can easily be adjusted to fit the talent available.
3. It is an offense in which individual freedom can be developed and encouraged.
4. It can also be a disciplined offense.
5. It has good offensive balance with the pivot-post man and two forwards in good position to score and in good position for offensive rebounding.
6. It has good defensive balance with two guards in position to make quick offensive thrusts and still be in position to get back on defense quickly.
7. The guards and forwards can be easily adjusted in their play to give more defensive or offensive thrust as the situation may demand.
8. It has much flexibility in styling, patterns, and options available.

Diagram 1-1 is a standard set-up for the Single Pivot-Post offense. The guards bring the ball down the floor about 12 to 15 feet apart. The forwards set up on a line about even with the free throw line extended, and back of it, in about 5 or 6 feet from the side line. The Pivot-Post player operates up and down the lane, his nearness to the basket being

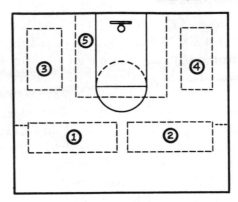

DIAGRAM 1-1

determined by his ability to score, hook shoot, and play as a feeder. The dotted line areas give the beginning operational areas of each position. From these positions the players begin moves that will lead to scoring opportunities. In all the diagrams for this offense the guards are numbered 1 and 2, the forwards are numbered 3 and 4, while the pivot-post player is numbered 5.

Diagram 1-2 shows the operational areas of No. 5—the pivot-post player—giving the positions to which he may maneuver to receive passes, and to screen (post) for teammates. No. 5 must time his maneuvers and movements so that they coincide with the moves and passes of his teammates. He must maneuver his defensive man behind him so that he can receive passes as he moves to the spots shown. He must also learn to take advantage of the defensive player who aggressively plays in front of him by reversing and taking a pass over the defensive player. No. 5 is the hub of the offense, and passes to him are very necessary for the offense to function as a Pivot-Post offense.

DIAGRAM 1-2

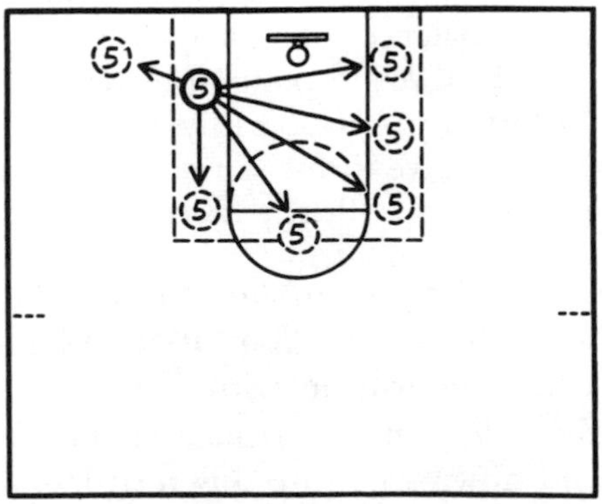

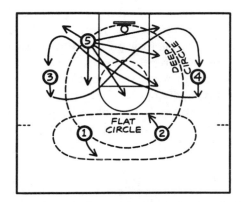

DIAGRAM 1-3

Diagram 1-3 illustrates that there is a definite circulation pattern for the guards and the forwards in the Single Pivot-Post offense. The guards No. 1 and No. 2 break and circulate in two general patterns—a deep circle and a flat circle as shown by the dotted circle patterns. The forwards break and circulate from their operational areas in a pattern similar to the figure 8 as shown by the solid lines for the general movements for No. 3 and No. 4. The pivot-post player No. 5 breaks and cuts for openings in his operational area as shown here which is in the area of the free throw lane.

REQUIREMENTS FOR THE POSITIONS IN THE OFFENSE

The ideal requirements for the positions in the Single Pivot-Post offense will be given here.

Guards

1. Must have speed.
2. The guards must be the quarterback type because they run the offense.
3. They must be able to drive.
4. They must be good passers.
5. They should be good shots 18 to 25 feet from the basket.
6. They must have a sense of defensive balance and defensive ability.

Forwards

1. Speed is desirable.
2. They must be good rebounders.
3. They should be good shots from the side areas and around 18 feet from the basket.

4. They must be very good at feeding the pivot-post players since their passing lanes to this player are the most advantageous, and most passes to him will come from the forward operational areas.

5. They must be able to drive the baseline area.

6. Their first requirement when they get the ball is to turn and face the basket and the pivot-post operational area.

7. To meet these requirements the forwards will usually be taller than the guards, and not as tall as the pivot-post player, but there can be exceptions to this.

The Pivot-Post Player

1. This player must be mentally tough and have a "mental set" required for the position.

2. He should be physically strong and be able to take physical punishment in his work around the backboards and the pivot-post position.

3. He must have the ability to come out with the ball in tough situations.

4. He should be the best rebounder.

5. If he is tall and big—it helps and the more the better.

6. He must be a good feeder to cutting teammates.

7. If he has a good hook shot, it helps. The more potent his scoring ability, the more versatile the attack can become.

OPERATIONAL MOVEMENTS OF THE PIVOT-POST PLAYER

The fundamental principle of the Pivot-Post offense is that one player will be stationed near the basket and free throw lane area and be operational in this area. This player will be the focal point of the offense. The extent to which he is the focal point will be determined by his abilities, versatility, and the talents of his teammates in their ability to use him as the wheel of the offense. Generally speaking this player is the tallest and largest player on the team, although there have been successful pivot-post players from 5'8" on up to the tallest in the game. He must be able to handle the physical wear and tear of close contact work that will ensue around the basket area and that will result from his being the center point of the offense. He must crash the backboards for rebounding work, be able to catch the ball and pass off under difficult conditions and at least be a scoring threat. The more he can score, the more versatile his position can become. He must have good judgment in when to pass to a cutting teammate, when to feint, when to withhold a pass, when to turn and shoot, or throw the ball back out to the mid-court area to open up the offense and start over again. There is no limit to what you can say the talents for this player should be. Most coaches have to settle for less than the maximum talents that could be used by a player in this position. Of course, if he is a good jumper, quick reacting, and a superb defensive player, it all adds to the utilization that can be made of him.

As the name of the position indicates, the pivot-post player in this offense can be used in a dual purpose capacity. The player will maneuver in the pivot-post operational area as shown in Diagrams 1-1, 1-2, and 1-3. He may operate as a pivot player and in this capacity as the focal point of the offense, the ball is passed to him ahead of cutting teammates who cut by him to free themselves of their defensive opponent and to gain a much needed one-step or a half-step advantage to receive a return pass for a scoring opportunity. This is often referred to as "ball-ahead-of-the-man" technique. The cutting teammate may also cut to areas other than by the pivot-post player as he finds opportunities to score by breaking to other areas (as will be shown by the diagraming of various options that may be run from the offense). Players cutting by the pivot-post player are not limited just to the passer. Most offenses using this style of play will cut two players by the pivot-post in what is called a "split-the-post" maneuver and some offenses will even break a third player by him. The offenses that cut two players by the pivot-post usually follow the pattern of requiring the player who passes the ball to the pivot-post player be the first cutter by following his pass, and that his teammate in the cutting play will be the player who had passed to him just before he forwarded the ball on to the pivot-post. In this type of play the pivot-post player operates chiefly as a *pivot* player.

In his second function as a pivot-post player the man in this position can operate as a *post* player. In this capacity he acts as a screener for cutting and dribbling teammates in order to free them for scoring opportunities around the free throw lane. This type of play is used more when the pivot-post player is less a scoring threat himself, when he cannot get open to receive passes for cutting teammates, and when the teammates are less skilled at passing him the ball in the area to set up the cutting play.

Maneuvering to get free for a pass in the free throw lane area and to time this maneuvering so as to coordinate with the moves of teammates and their passing efforts becomes a very necessary skill for the pivot-post player. He must maneuver his defensive opponent so that the latter will be behind him when he receives the ball and the play is about to begin. Defensive players become clever and are difficult to maneuver into this position as they become more skilled and receive help from teammates. The pivot-post player must vary his movements, and work in a variety of moves, fakes, and feints to out-maneuver the defensive players. Usually the most success can be obtained by moving in the direction away from the ball, and then doubling back quickly for an opening in the area where a pass can be received in front of the defensive player. Actually, fakes and maneuvers should be away from the ball and the move to secure position and the pass will be toward the ball, and timed to synchronize with the passing and moves of the teammates who are working to get the ball to him. Very seldom can the pivot-post player assume a set position and receive the ball, for most defensive players will not remain behind him. All of this requires a lot of work on timing, maneuvering, and teamwork so that this player can receive the ball in an advantageous position for feeding cutting teammates or for converting the score himself.

OPERATIONAL MOVEMENTS OF THE FORWARDS

The forwards in this offense function in the area behind the free throw line extended, about two strides from the sideline and all the way to the baseline. Their operational areas, general cutting lanes, and circulation patterns are also shown in Diagrams 1-1, 1-2, and 1-3. In addition to the requirements listed for the players in this position, they are expected to be more skilled at cutting and driving for scoring opportunities than the pivot-post player. The better these players are at fulfilling the techniques required in their position, the better and more versatile the offense can be. They are also expected to be able to crash the boards for rebounds, and to help the guards in securing defensive balance when needed. Their moves, cuts, and patterns of play will be explained as we outline the offensive plays that can be run from this offense.

OPERATIONAL MOVEMENTS OF THE GUARDS

The two guards No. 1 and No. 2 in this offense will start their moves from the operational areas as shown in the first three diagrams. It is not necessary that they be the smaller players, but in accordance with the requirements listed for these positions, usually the smaller, more fleet-of-foot, and versatile and maneuverable will be the guards in this offense. They should be better outside shooters, good passers, dribblers, feeders, cutters, and have defensive sense and ability. They start all plays by bringing the ball up the floor and initiating all action when the forwards and the pivot-post man get in their operational areas.

BASIC PLAY PATTERNS

To start the offense, the guards bring the ball down the floor and all players form in their operational areas. The two guards, always numbered

No. 1 and No. 2 in this offense, play about the width of the free throw lane apart so that they will always be in position to help each other out in case of trouble. The offense can be started in a number of ways, but always this offense has the focal point upon the pivot-post player with the intent of getting the ball to him. Other options are possible and desirable of course. If the defense concentrates upon preventing the pass into the pivot-post player to the extent that it becomes almost impossible, they should have to pay the price. Option plays which bypass this player should then be possible so as to exploit any weakness elsewhere caused by an over-concentration upon the pivot-post player by the defense. The whole offense must not rest completely upon a forcing pass into the pivot-post man, or it will crumble on nights when the defense takes this pass away.

There are many plays and patterns that can be run from the formation, and the offense can be adjusted easily to fit the situation presented by the defense. While most of the plays presented for this offense are set up for operation against the man-to-man defense, the offense can with slight variations and adjustments in position of the players, operate equally as well against zone defenses, or combination defenses. Offenses that are to be run against zone defenses are treated elsewhere in this book and are considered as separate offenses.

One famous high school coach had a good name for this offense when he referred to it as the "1001 play," because he said, "There are 1001 options you can run from this play."

In Diagram 1-4, the ball starts with No. 2 who dribbles into an exchange with No. 1. No. 1 taking the ball dribbles over to his right and passes into forward No. 4 who has maneuvered free for a pass in his operational area. No. 5 has maneuvered his defensive man so as to get free for a pass from No. 4 just as No. 4 receives the ball. No. 4 passes into No. 5 and starts a quick break "over the top" of No. 5 and close by him. However, in order to secure a split over the pivot-post, No. 4 goes into a series of *staccato* steps to slow up enough for No. 1 who first breaks to his left, to veer to his right and sharply behind No. 4, thus securing the possibility of a double screen on the "split" over the pivot-post player No. 5. No. 5 can feed either No. 4 or No. 1 if open, or he may maneuver for an individual opening after the cutters have gone by, or look to No. 3, or No. 2 for a possible pass-out and to set up the offense again. Several options are possible from this play. In starting the exchange, No. 2, after handing off to No. 1, could do a roll-out and a cut, down the center for a possible return pass on the deep circle pattern, or he can fake a roll-out and drop back to the flat circle and let No. 1 carry the option to No. 4. After passing

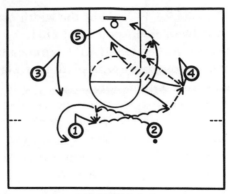

DIAGRAM 1-4

to No. 4, No. 1 could break sharply in for a return pass or a possible delayed "split," with No. 4 passing to No. 5 and cutting sharply behind No. 1 and over the top of No. 5 with all the options possible here. A continuity series can be worked out from this one option and is given as Phase 2 in Diagram 1-5.

Diagram 1-5 is a continuation of Diagram 1-4, giving Phase 2, or a continuity pattern. If neither No. 4 or No. 1 are open as they "split-the-post" and No. 5 has no opening himself, he quickly shifts position from one side of the lane to the other by a dribble, and sets up a pivot-post position there with No. 3 and No. 2 working a "split" over this post position. The same options are possible from here. (In all the diagrams, if the play is run to the right, the same play may be run to the left.) No. 1 continues on his cut through the deep circle, and back to the defensive

DIAGRAM 1-5

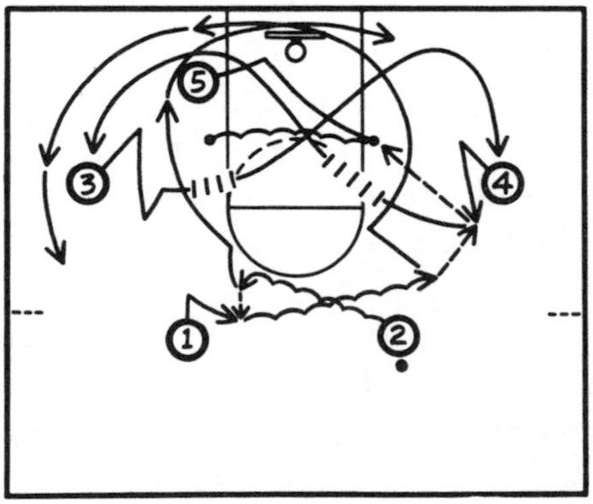

position, and No. 3 and No. 4 have, in actuality, done a figure 8 in an exchange of positions. After the second "split" over the pivot-post, No. 2 would quickly return to his operational areas. If a shot goes up, the pivot-post player and the forwards Nos. 5, 4, and 3 crash to positions for rebounds.

Diagram 1-6 is a continuation of Diagrams 1-4 and 1-5, giving a possible option to the split-the-post series. Players No. 2 and No. 1 start with an exchange to get the defense moving with No. 2 dribbling to his left, handing off the ball to No. 1 moving to his right. No. 1 then passes to forward No. 4 who comes up to receive the ball in his operational area, after shaking his defensive player. No. 4 immediately turns and passes the ball into No. 5 who has first maneuvered away and freed himself for a pass along the free throw lane. No. 4 follows his pass, but cuts his stride into *staccato* steps so that No. 2 may after faking a drive to his left, cut sharply off the back of No. 4 in a "split-the-post" maneuver close "over-

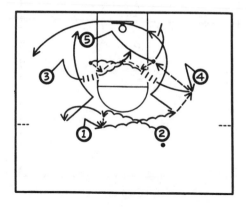

DIAGRAM 1-6

the-top" of No. 5. In this option No. 5 flips the ball to No. 4 who dribbles across the lane and now sets a pivot-post position on the opposite side of the lane. Forward No. 3 and guard No. 2 now work a "split-the-post" maneuver over No. 4 in the same manner as was done on the opposite side over No. 5. No. 4 passes off to No. 3 who may take any scoring opportunity available to him. No. 4 could have passed to No. 2 or he could pass to No. 1 who, in returning to the guard position, could be a third cutter over No. 4 for options, or he could take other options or regroup the offense. No. 5, after passing off to No. 4 rolls down the lane to be in rebound position, if the ball goes up on a shot.

Diagram 1-7 is another of the many options available in this offense. The guards can work split-the-post maneuvers for scoring opportunities. When the ball is passed to the pivot-post player, well positioned in the outer half of the free throw circle, this is the signal for a guard "split." When the guards split, the forwards must come back to the mid-court area to cover for defensive balance. No. 1 dribbles to his left to get a better passing angle as No. 5 maneuvers for position in the outside portion of the free-throw circle. After passing to No. 5, No. 1 fakes straight in and then breaks to his right, going into a *staccato* movement to get timing so that No. 2 can cut just behind him as they both break close by No. 5 for the "split." No. 5 has the option of passing to anyone open, or turning for scoring opportunities himself, or he can pass out to No. 3 or No. 4, and the offense can regroup. Another option is for No. 3 and No. 4 to also work a "split" over No. 5, if no opening comes from the guard split, in a "double-split" maneuver.

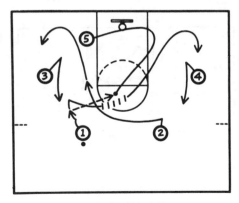

DIAGRAM 1-7

As in Diagram 1-8, the forwards have the best passing angle, and most of the time the ball will be moved from the forward to the pivot-post player, but the guards can maneuver for good passing angles and move the ball to him. Here No. 2 maneuvers to his right, and finding No. 5 open after maneuvering his defensive man behind him, passes into him. No. 2 and No. 4 now work a "split" move over No. 5 with No. 2 first faking a move to his left, then sharply right into a *staccato* movement of steps so that No. 4 can cut closely behind him, and both cut closely over the top of No. 5. No. 5 has the option of passing to either No. 2 or No. 4 as the opening may present itself. Two other options are very possible here. As soon as No. 5 secures the ball, he looks to his right for a possible option

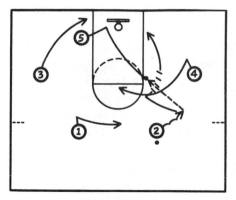

DIAGRAM 1-8

of passing to No. 3, who cuts the baseline in this situation any time the ball comes to No. 5. This often presents a good scoring opportunity. Another option possible in this play is for No. 1 to continue as the third breaker over the top of No. 5 if neither No. 2 or No. 4 are open. This presents a three player scissor movement by the pivot-post man and adds to scoring possibilities.

Diagram 1-9 begins a movement called the guard-inside series, and it works around the Pivot-Post but in a delayed movement that presents other options before the ball is passed into No. 5. Nos. 1 and 2 maneuver and exchange as shown, No. 1 moving out to his right securing a good passing angle, passes the ball into No. 4 who has freed himself for the pass in his operational area. No. 1 now has two options he can make. He can move straight for the basket for a quick return pass if open, or he can follow his pass and throw an inside screen on No. 4's defensive man.

DIAGRAM 1-9

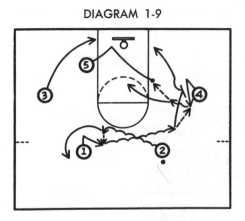

As No. 1 screens on the inside, No. 4 dribbles sharply toward the inside
and close behind No. 1. Here he may shoot, or pass to No. 1, who as soon
as No. 4 dribbles far enough to get a defensive switch, rolls and cuts for
the basket for a possible opening, or he may pass to No. 5 who is now in
position to pivot-post for him. Passing to No. 5, No. 4 cuts by him for
a possible return pass and its options, or No. 5 may pass to No. 1 rolling
in, or to No. 3 cutting the baseline on the opposite side. Any of the options
are available that have been shown in previous diagrams. The difference
here is that the guard follows his pass to the forward for a screen and
roll-off option, which can be followed by a play to the pivot-post man with
all its options. Remember all plays run to the right can also be run to
the left.

Diagram 1-10, a continuation of Diagram 1-9, shows how the screen
and roll-off maneuver between Nos. 1 and 4 would be worked, with No. 5
being left out of the play entirely, and securing position for the rebound.
Nos. 1 and 2 maneuver on an exchange and No. 1 taking the pass moves
to his right to pass the ball into No. 4 who frees himself for the pass in
his operational area. No. 1 following the pass screens to the inside of No.
4 and on the defensive man X4 who is guarding No. 4. As No. 4 dribbles
closely by and behind No. 1, No. 1 rolls-off or cuts out to split the defense
and to get an opening for a return pass from No. 4 as shown here. The
timing on the screen, dribble, roll-off, and pass must be perfect, and
requires much practice. The most successful pass in this situation will
usually be a sharp bounce pass by the defensive player who switches to
No. 4 and one that reaches No. 1 before the defensive switch can be fully
executed, thereby giving No. 1 a lead on the defensive player switching

DIAGRAM 1-10

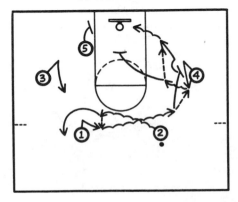

to him. A sharp, but soft lob pass by No. 4's defensive player will be the next best pass selection for this play, especially when the bounce pass is well faked prior to its execution. No. 4 can also execute options of shooting from behind the screen or pass to Nos. 5, 3, or 2.

Diagram 1-11 shows the guard-outside series. This option varies from that given in Diagrams 1-9 and 1-10 only in that the guard after passing to a forward, follows his pass to the outside. Here Nos. 1 and 2 maneuver, and No. 1 moving the ball to the right, passes the ball to No. 4, following on a cut outside of No. 4, or between No. 4 and the

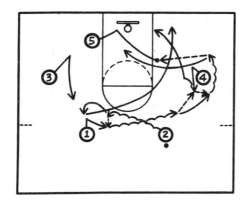

DIAGRAM 1-11

sideline. Several options and opportunities are possible from here. No. 4 may turn and face the inside and maneuver on his hope of passing into No. 5. He may also hand-off to No. 1 cutting to the outside. From here No. 1 can drive, shoot, possibly pass to No. 4 on a roll-off move to the basket (see Diagram 1-12), or he can pass into No. 5, as shown here. Passing into No. 5 on the pivot-post, he can work a "split" over No. 5 with No. 4. Here also guard No. 2 could cut over the top of No. 5 bringing a third man in on the split series in which case No. 3 must cover the midcourt area for defensive balance. Individual freedom should be allowed to develop all the possibilities from the play. This play is shown moving to the right. The same play and all its options can also move to the left.

Diagram 1-12 is a continuation of Diagram 1-11. An option available on this series is the moves that can be made between the guards and forwards in screens and roll-off moves cutting into the basket, and then using the pivot-post player in a delayed move by working the ball to him and

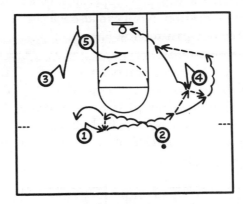

DIAGRAM 1-12

moving in "splits" over the top. In this diagram No. 4 handed the ball back to No. 1 cutting to the outside who could whip up a quick change of pace on a drive for the basket that would free him for scoring possibilities or he could dribble for timing and look to pass to No. 4 on a roll-off maneuver that would "split" the defense as shown here. If he should find that No. 4 was not open, then No. 5 could maneuver his defensive man behind him for an opening, and a pass from No. 1, and then No. 1 could "split-the-post with either No. 2 or No. 3 for possible scoring opportunities.

In Diagram 1-13 guards No. 1 and No. 2 maneuver and cross for an opening and to get the defense moving. No. 1 clears out on a dribble to the right and passes the ball into No. 4 who shakes his defensive man for the opening in his operational area. No. 1 following his pass to the out-

DIAGRAM 1-13

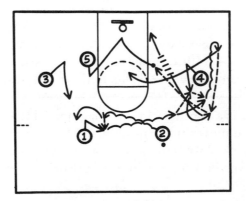

side receives the ball back from No. 4. No. 1, dribbling, finds no opening or opportunity to pass into No. 5, pivots or turns to the outside and passes to No. 4, who after handing off to No. 1 previously, had taken two or three strides toward the mid-court area. Now No. 4 and No. 1 can move the ball back and forth again in a shuttle movement, if the ball cannot be passed into No. 5. The object of the move is to pass the ball into No. 5 as soon as he can maneuver his defensive man behind him and be in position to receive a pass. The pass into No. 5 could come from either No. 4 or No. 1, after which they would work a "split" over the pivot-post for further opportunities. The third cutter or split could also be brought in on this play, being either No. 2 or No. 3 as the opportunity presents itself, or according to the talents of the players. The play can go either right or left.

Diagram 1-14 shows the inside-outside series. The offense must have scoring opportunities that come from situations other than when the ball is passed into the pivot-post player. This will take the pressure off the pivot-post player, and will prevent the offense from dependence upon a forcing pass into this position. The inside-outside series or play is often referred to as "the second guard through" play. In this diagram, Nos. 1 and 2 maneuver and No. 1 moving out to the right, passes into No. 4 and breaks inside No. 4 faking a screen and roll out, and then moves on through rapidly. No. 4 dribbles close behind No. 1, and No. 5, not being open, clears the area to the opposite side. No. 4 now continues his dribble toward the free throw lane. He may take any opportunity available to him and can drive on through if open. If not open, he maneuvers his defensive man as deep toward the basket as possible, and then pivots forming a pivot-post position. No. 2, after having passed off to No. 1, has maneuvered in the mid-court area. Now, faking to his left to maneuver

DIAGRAM 1-14

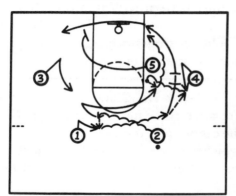

his defensive man into position, and to get the timing, cuts sharply by
No. 4 for a hand-off pass, and a possible drive for the basket. If timed
properly, the explosiveness of this situation usually finds the No. 2 guard
free for scoring opportunities.

In Diagram 1-15 the play known by many as the "Sucker Play" and
the "Blind Pig" is another option used to take the pressure off the pivot-
post player, and to give additional scoring opportunities. No. 1 moving
in a dribble to his left cannot feed the ball to No. 5, who fades out of the
area. No. 1 then goes into an inside shuttle move with No. 3. No. 3 dribbles the ball out and passes the ball into No. 4 who during the previous
moves has made a jab to the baseline and then breaks quickly to the outer
half of the free throw circle to receive the pass from No. 3. No. 2, whose

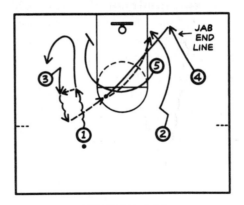

DIAGRAM 1-15

defensive man will usually turn his head just enough to watch the ball
movement, jabs to his left, and breaks to the right of the free throw lane
area. No. 4 can feed him the ball anywhere he is open for the pass. The
play carries a continuity pattern with it, and if No. 2 is not open, then
No. 3 can jab step to his left, and break close by No. 4 for an opening, or
he can go into a "split" pattern with No. 1 over the top of No. 4 for
possible opening for the scoring opportunity.

In Diagram 1-16 players No. 2 and No. 4 are working the outside
shuttle pattern and, after receiving the ball from No. 4 on an outside
move, No. 2 finds he cannot pass the ball into No. 5 in the pivot-post area.
No. 2, or No. 4, whichever one happens to be in this position after the
shuttle move, passes the ball out to No. 1 who has followed the play to

his right in a balancing and adjusting move. No. 1 passes the ball quickly to No. 3 who has made a jab move to the baseline, and then quickly breaking to the outer half of the free throw circle to receive the pass from No. 1. No. 1 quickly follows his pass breaking close by No. 3 to rub off his defensive man. No. 3 feeds the ball to No. 1 and he drives quickly for the opening. No. 3 may take the options of turning and maneuvering for other openings, if No. 1 is not open.

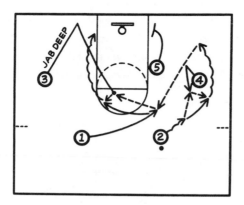

DIAGRAM 1-16

Diagram 1-17 illustrates a double pick or screen for two players and features the pivot-post player in a true *post* roll. The play can be called by name or number, but in the move No. 2 starts the play on a "guard outside" move by passing the ball into No. 4, following the pass and receiving a pass-back or a hand-off from No. 4. No. 2 dribbles toward the baseline, and No. 5 and No. 4 both move to the outer half of the free

DIAGRAM 1-17

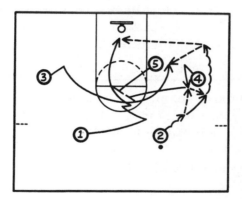

throw circle to set a double post screen for first No. 1 and then No. 3 who scissor in moves by the screen. No. 2 can pass to whichever one is open or relay the ball back out to Nos. 4 or 5 on roll-off moves if the first two cutters are not open.

Many teams break three players over the top of the pivot-post player in a three-way "split" (see Diagram 1-18). It has certain advantages in that it affords more possible scoring opportunities and a possible double pick or screen move around the pivot-post player which can be very effective. It has the possible weakness of leaving the team with a weaker defensive balance at times, and of possibly creating too much congestion around pivot-post player. In Diagram 1-18, No. 2 passes to No. 4 who relays the ball into No. 5 in the pivot-post area. After passing to No. 4,

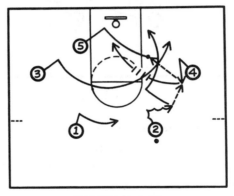

DIAGRAM 1-18

No. 2 veers to his left and as No. 4 cuts by No. 5, giving his *staccato* steps if necessary to get timing on the move, No. 2 then cuts sharply off the back of No. 4. Either may be open, but No. 3 has timed his move out across the free throw lane so that he will be a third cutter by No. 5, but he first will move off No. 4's back, and close enough to get a possible double screen off the position created by Nos. 4 and 5. No. 5 takes the best option.

Diagram 1-19 shows one player breaking by the pivot-post ahead of the ball followed by the ball ahead of the man and a "split" by two players. No. 2 moving to his right passes the ball into No. 4 and follows the pass to the outside. Just before No. 2 reaches No. 4, No. 4 flips the ball back to No. 2 who comes to a stop with the ball, with a dribble option remain-

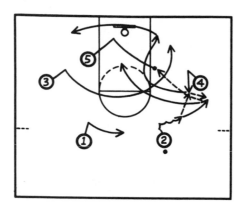

DIAGRAM 1-19

ing. After passing the ball back to No. 2, No. 4 turns and cuts over the top of No. 5, who has maneuvered into a pass receiving position on the right side of the lane, and near the free throw line. The first opening that No. 2 looks for is a pass to No. 4 as he cuts off No. 5, and a high pass may catch him sometimes beyond No. 5, and deep, or sometimes a sharp pass just behind No. 5 and to the right of the lane will find No. 4 open. If No. 4 is not open, No. 2 now has a dribble to maneuver with and he may drive for an opening or he may pass into No. 5 and work a "split" ma-neuver over No. 5 with No. 3. This particular sequence has been featured by many championship teams.

2

The Double Pivot-Post Offense

Once the Single Pivot-Post offense became a popular functioning reality as a basketball offense, it was only a matter of time until the *Double* Pivot-Post would be established by an ingenious coach or player. It was almost a repetition of the biblical story of creation—first there was one, and then there were two. No one seems to take credit for its origin or development in the annals of basketball, but by the early 1930's several prominent teams were using offenses that could be classed as a Double Pivot-Post offense. It has continued to be popular and to have wide usage up to the present time.

If one were to speculate as to the origin of the Double Pivot-Post offense, it probably would be safe to assume that its birth came about as the result of a coach having developed a good reserve player for the pivot-post position in the Single Pivot-Post offense. The reserve player may have developed so well that the coach soon found himself in a dilemma as to which player to play and finally solved the situation by devising an offense with a double pivot-post function. It could have also resulted from a coach or a team having two very fine pivot-post players and, not being anxious to have one such fine player ride the bench while only one played, thus developed the idea of placing the two players near the basket to operate as pivot-post players with the other three smaller and more versatile players maneuvering on the outside and working the ball into these two basketball giants for scoring opportunities.

Regardless of the origin of the Double Pivot-Post offense, it is a formation that adapts itself well to many variations and styles of play. Many, many possibilities can be worked out from the offense and it adapts itself well to talent at hand.

As with the Single Pivot-Post offense, the Double Pivot-Post offense contributed its share to legislative processes whereby the rules makers passed the three-second lane rule and later widened the lane to 12 feet. Certainly, with two offensive men stationed in this area and both maneuvering for position with their defensive opponents, the play tended to be doubly rough. The development of the Double Pivot-Post offense may have been the clincher to the legislative processes that invoked the above-mentioned rules.

ADVANTAGES OF THE DOUBLE PIVOT-POST OFFENSE

1. For the team that has two large and very fine pivot-post players, it provides a means of taking full advantage of both their talents.
2. It gives added scoring opportunities from the pivot area.
3. It places two men that should be the best rebounders in position for rebounds.
4. It gives the team stronger defensive balance with three men out and in position to get back quickly on defense and foil any fast break attempt.
5. It is an offense in which individual freedom can be developed and encouraged.
6. With three guards to bring the ball down the floor, there should be fewer problems in getting the ball up the floor and in position to trigger the offensive play patterns.
7. The offense has much flexibility in styling, patterns, and options available and lends itself well to adapting the offense to the talent of players available.
8. If the team has no big players or tall players available for the pivot-post position, two medium sized players or smaller players can be worked into this Double Pivot-Post offense, featuring more speed and maneuverability to a good advantage.
9. The Double Pivot-Post offense can incorporate two basic principles of pivot-post play in the offense in the same play and at the same time. These principles are "ball ahead of the man" and "man ahead of the ball." With two pivot-post men, these two concepts can occur at the same time on the same play for more potent scoring opportunities.

DISADVANTAGES OF THE DOUBLE PIVOT-POST OFFENSE

1. Positioning two big men in the pivot area may clog the center lane and reduce driving opportunities. In fact, some coaches dropped this offense

when the officiating became strict in calling charging fouls on offensive players who were frequently finding this area jammed as they attempted to drive.

2. Some coaches claim that with three players out, this offense does not give the offensive balance and punch that a good offense ought to have.
3. With only two players near the basket, in some situations it could leave the team weak in rebounding strength.

In actual application of play, there are two types of Double Pivot-Post offenses. One is called the "Tight" pivot-post play, or the "Close" play. In this offense two men are placed in close to the free throw lane and they operate with screens, shooting, feeding teammates, and rebounding for scoring opportunities. This offense usually features two bigger, taller and slower men and they work for close-in shooting, screening, and rebounding. The other type is often called the "Open" double pivot-post play. In this offense the pivot-post men are placed wider and further from the free throw lane. It would make for a more open game, more cutting and driving opportunities, with more one-on-one plays and inside screens. Smaller men can usually be used in the pivot-post positions in this type of play to a better advantage because they are more maneuverable. This style also affords an opportunity to use one big tall man and a small man who plays the pivot position well in a dual pivot-post combination with good results. The wider placement of the men on the pivot-post positions weakens rebounding strength, but it affords an ideal opportunity for "flash" pivot-post plays which can be more effective than the more jammed double pivot-post position when both players are in tight. Also, with the pivot-post men wider, the angle for feeding passes to the post men from the front and sides offers better possibilities.

In this chapter both the "tight" and the "open" pivot-post offenses will be explained. Diagram 2-1 gives the standard set-up for the "Tight" Pivot-Post offense. Diagram 2-2 gives the operational area for each player in the "Open" Double Pivot-Post offense.

In Diagram 2-1, guards 1, 2, and 3 begin their moves from the operational areas shown. They may incorporate any variety of moves that will be explained later to get the offense moving. They may go into a three-man weave pattern, working the ball until they move it into one of the pivot-post men, or secure some other scoring opportunity. They might also work the ball down the sides, securing better passing angles for feeding the pivot-post players.

Players 4 and 5 are the pivot-post players. Here they are shown in the "Tight" positions. These two players will use all the arts known to the pivot-post player to get open within their operational area. They

can scissor with each other and double back to get open ahead of their
defensive men and work splits or other maneuvers (as later diagrams will
show) for scoring opportunities.

In Diagram 2-2, the guards again are 1, 2, and 3. Usually No. 1, the
player in the center, starts the offensive moves and so becomes the "trigger" man. He needs to be more of the quarterback type player. Players
No. 1, 2, and 3 dribble and weave in a semi-circle to get the offense moving. Nos. 4 and 5 are the pivot-post players. Here they are shown in the

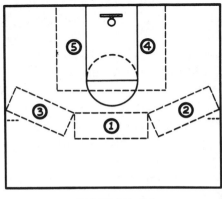

DIAGRAM 2-1

DIAGRAM 2-2

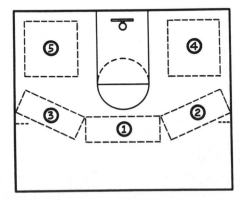

"Open" or wide pivot-post positions. From these operational areas they flash the pivot area for openings and/or scissor with each other to secure openings for passes from the outside.

Diagram 2-3 gives the circulation pattern of the players in the pivot-post offense. The three guards, Nos. 1, 2, and 3, drive, cut, and circulate in two general patterns, a flat circle and the deep circle shown by the dotted lines. There will be more flat circle moves by the guards in this offense than in the Single Pivot-Post offense because the guards will maneuver in a weave style of movements more, to work the ball into the the two pivot-post men. The two pivot-post men will circulate in moves shown by the solid lines in what might be termed scissor movements, using each other as screens and in exchanging positions in maneuvers to get free to receive the ball for pivot-post play. Also in this offense, the two post men sometimes start their moves close to the basket, or in what is called a "deep" or "low" position. At other times they may play the positions as shown by the dotted numbers, or in what is called a "high" position which is farther from the basket.

REQUIREMENTS FOR THE POSITIONS IN THE OFFENSE

The ideal player requirements for the various positions in this offense will vary from the positions in other offenses.

Guards

1. The No. 1 player must be the true quarterback type, for most plays are initiated by him. He is sometimes referred to as the "trigger" man.
2. Players No. 2 and 3 could have the combined qualities of the guards

DIAGRAM 2-3

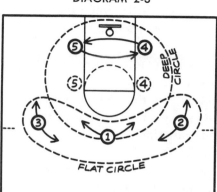

and forwards as given in the Single Pivot-Post offense. They have often been referred to as "wingmen" and as "pinchers."

3. They must have speed.
4. They must be able to drive.
5. They must be good passers.
6. They should be good outside shooters.
7. A sense of defensive balance and ability is a requisite of the positions.
8. If at least one of these outside players has the ability to crash the boards with the double-pivot men, it will help counter-balance a weakness of the offense.
9. All the players in the guard or outside positions must be able to deftly feed the pivot-post men.

The Pivot-Post Players

1. If both players have all the requirements listed for the pivot-post player in the Single Pivot-Post offense, it would help.
2. They both should be good rebounders.
3. They both should have a good hook shot.
4. It would be an advantage if the pivot-post player playing the right side of the floor were left-handed, and the one playing the left side of the floor were right-handed. If this were true, both could move toward the middle of the floor with their best shots.
5. They should have good hands.
6. They should be good jumpers.
7. They should be deft feeders of cutting teammates.

OPERATIONAL MOVEMENTS OF THE PIVOT-POST PLAYERS

To begin the offense the two pivot-post players will station themselves on each side of the free throw lane. Their nearness to the basket and distance from the lane will depend upon a number of factors, such as their ability to hook shoot, their size, maneuverability, and in some situations, the pressures of the defense. The various ways in which they can set up their operational areas are shown in Diagrams 2-1, 2-2, and 2-3. Sometimes they will be in the "tight" positions. At other times they will be in the "open" positions, or the "high" positions, depending upon the talent of the pivot-post players and their teammates, what they can do in a given situation, and sometimes whatever the defensive pressures may dictate.

In maneuvering to get open for passes from the outside teammates or guards, the double pivot-post players need to synchronize their movements to keep from jamming the cutting lanes and to be able to time their receiving moves with the passing efforts of the guards. This will require a lot of practice to develop the precise timing necessary. They may move individually in their efforts to free themselves for openings, or they may use a series of scissor movements back and forth across the free throw lane, creating screening opportunities for each other to get open for passes from the guards and to set up either the "man ahead of the ball" move or the "ball ahead of the man" move, or both. As in the Single Pivot-Post offense, when the ball is received by one of the pivot-post players in the operational area, a "split" maneuver is worked over the top of the pivot-post player. He may feed the open teammate or maneuver for an opening for himself. If no opening develops, the ball can be returned to one of the outside players and the offense can be started over again.

The Double Pivot-Post offense has the advantage of being able to feature both the possibilities of "man ahead of the ball" and "ball ahead of the man" at the same time or on the same move or play. This can be done by breaking a player by the second pivot-post player as the ball is passed into his teammate. It could also be handled by having the pivot-post player that is free move out to the opposite area and screen for a cutting teammate just as the ball is received by his teammate pivot-post player. This action would immediately be followed by teammates "splitting" the pivot-post player that has just received the ball.

It must be remembered that the pivot-post players have two chief functions. They are (1) to score, and (2) to feed cutting teammates. If they cannot perform these two functions well, they are worthless. It is also necessary when two pivot-post players are used that their playing technique include a strong "follow-in" for rebounds on ALL shots.

In order to score they must develop a variety of shots, including a good hook shot and a good jump shot combined with a variety of fakes, feints, and maneuvers to get open for opportunities to score. Feeding passes to cutting teammates becomes a necessary technique. These players must master a variety of flip passes, hand-offs, bounce passes, back bounces, over-the-shoulder, underhand, and cross flip pass techniques, even behind the back passes, that will enable them to deftly feed cutting teammates. They must also learn to assume a good stable base for protecting the ball so that, as teammates cut by them, opponents will not be able to wrest or slap the ball away from them.

OPERATIONAL MOVEMENTS OF THE GUARDS

The three guards are sometimes called the outside players, or rear court players. They bring the ball down the court to set up the offense and start their moves from the operational areas as shown in Diagrams 2-1 and 2-2. Their general circulation and cutting patterns are shown in Diagram 2-3.

These players may well combine the qualities required of guards and forwards in the Single Pivot-Post offense, but at least one of them should be the complete guard type and have the complete quarterback qualities, because this player (the one shown in the No. 1 position) will initiate nearly all plays. This offense can function very well also if ALL these players are of the pure guard type player. If the quarterback, No. 1, should be a tall player it could be an advantage to him in his passing and functioning as a "trigger" man in initiating the plays of the offense.

These players will continuously drive toward the basket, especially Nos. 2 and 3, and at least one of them should be back at all times ready for the defensive protection. All of these players, even while on offensive thrusts, should be conscious of their backcourt defensive responsibilities. They should thoroughly understand and be the masters of give-and-go plays, screening moves, split-the-post maneuvers, stops, starts, change of direction and change of pace tactics. When openings present themselves, they must be able to exploit the opportunity.

These players may start the offense by a weaving movement or by give-and-go tactics. Various trigger moves and options can be developed as shown by the diagramed plays that follow. The attack is developed largely by working the ball to one of the pivot-post men so that the outside players can drive and cut for the basket. These players must contribute their share of scoring balance to the team effort, from both outside and inside. If they are not effective scorers, the defense can collapse and double team the pivot-post players, thereby hampering their effectiveness. The outside players may drift laterally and deeper toward the baseline in meeting passes, and in setting up the offense. They should be very careful in feeding the pivot-post players directly from the rear court. Such a feed should find the pivot-post man moving. In feeding from the side areas they will have a better passing angle, but should always remember to concentrate upon the opponent guarding the pivot-post man and feed to the side away from the defensive player.

BASIC PLAY PATTERNS

The guards, Nos. 1, 2, and 3, bring the ball down the floor and, along with the two pivot players, form in their operational areas to set up the offense. There should be no trouble bringing the ball down the floor with three guards in the pattern to help out if any trouble develops. Usually in this type of offense one of the players assumes the chief responsibility for bringing the ball down the floor and the other two players give him help as needed. Some coaches prefer not to have two or three players bring the ball down the floor to set up the offense, but would rather rely on one good ballhandler to do this, securing help only when needed. These coaches claim fewer interceptions with one ballhandler doing the chore while the other players clear out for him, leaving him, if possible, with a one-on-one situation to get the ball into the needed operational area where an offense can be generated. Other coaches prefer to have all three players helping bring the ball upcourt, claiming fewer errors occur with this system.

The focal point of this offense is always the two pivot-post players with the intent of working the ball into one of these players unless another opening or scoring opportunity occurs. The offense is easily adapted to meet the talents of the players on the team and it can be easily adjusted to meet various defensive alignments that will be thrown up against it. It can even be changed very easily to be run against zone defenses or combination defenses.

The double pivot-post players must be cautious not to clog up the middle when an outside teammate secures a driving opportunity. When this happens they must clear very quickly to get out of the way of driving teammates. This clogging and jamming situation can develop especially with the tight formation where the double pivot-post men play close to the free throw lane. It takes a great deal of deftness and know-how on their part to know when and how to "clear out" of the area so as not to jam a move by one of the outside players. Constant harping and working on this can help the double pivot-post men in this development. Some coaches dropped this offense when the offensive drivers were charged with fouls for making contact with the defensive man when they drove into this jammed area. Today, with the added jump shot opportunities available for the double pivot-post players, this offense is being used more.

The offense can start in any number of ways, but in Diagram 2-4 No. 1 starts on a dribble weave to his left to get the defense moving. No. 3, drifting vertically toward the baseline, fakes a drive through, then reverses back to receive the ball on a double exchange or a hand-off from No. 1. Now No. 3 dribbles toward the middle, feeling the defense out and constantly watching the movements of No. 4 and No. 5. No. 2 fakes deep to his right and, getting open, comes back to receive a pass from No. 3. Nos. 4 and 5 have pulled a scissor move with No. 5 faking deep across the lane and No. 4 screening for No. 5, who breaks out sharply off the screen to receive a pass from No. 2. Nos. 2 and 3 now do a split over No. 5 with No. 2 faking to his right, then veering to his left and doing a series of *staccato* steps to get the timing so that No. 3, who first fakes to his left, can veer right and break closely off the back for a good screen. With correct timing and moves, one of these players should be open. No. 5 will feed the open man and, if none are open, he can return the ball to the outside to No. 1, who can start the offense over. No. 5 should also be alert

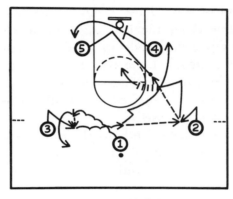

DIAGRAM 2-4

DIAGRAM 2-5

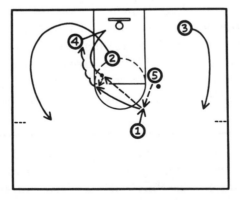

for the possibility of No. 1 being a third cutter and to the possibility of being able to catch No. 4 for an opening along the baseline, No. 4 having peeled out from the screen with No. 5 for a possible opening that might come from a guard who has relaxed his defensive efforts. All players on this move should be alert for drives or possible stops and jump shots off this play. Diagram 2-5 gives a continuance and a follow-up possible from this play.

After running the play shown in Diagram 2-4, if there are no openings, the players arrive at the positions shown in Diagram 2-5. No. 2 continues on through and clears out and No. 3 clears out to the right also. No. 2 could come off No. 4 for a possible opening, from No. 5, or No. 1, who receives the ball on the outside from No. 5, after other options have failed. Now, No. 1 could pass to No. 2 for a possible opening around No. 4 or, if this option does not materialize, then No. 4 breaks to the position shown, either to receive a pass from No. 1 or to serve as a "pinched-post" for No. 1 dribbling by him. In this diagram, No. 1 passes to No. 4 and cuts sharply by him for a return pass and a drive for the basket. He should be open.

Numbers 1, 2, and 3 can work in a weave pattern until an opening occurs. As shown in Diagram 2-6, they should drift vertically toward the

DIAGRAM 2-6

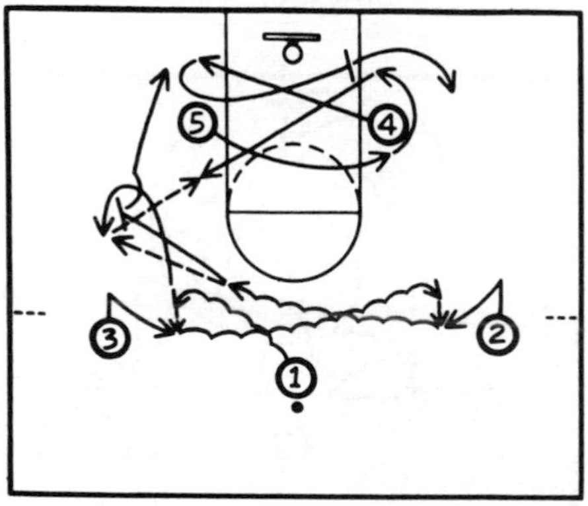

baseline before breaking back out to receive a hand-off. Otherwise, the defense will force them more toward mid-court line all the time and this is not desirable. Caution should be used also in passing into the pivot-post position from the center of the floor. The passing angle from here is poor and the defense can drift off more to deflect passes. Only if the pivot-post man is moving sharply toward the ball and the defense is tight, should a pass be attempted from here. Here the guards dribble weave and the pivot-post players scissor until No. 2, dribbling toward No. 1 who has drifted or faked vertically toward the baseline, passes to him, and moves inside him for a screen. No. 1 catches No. 5 off a scissor screen movement just off the edge of the screen. No. 1 and No. 2 do a "split" move over the post.

The third man can be brought into the Double Pivot-Post offense just as in any other "split-the-post" series. In Diagram 2-7 No. 1 starts the offense by a move to his left. (Remember any play shown moving to one side can also be run to the opposite side.) No. 1 passes off to No. 3 who moves to the center of the floor and passes the ball to No. 2 who has shaken loose in his area. No. 2 forwards the ball into No. 5 who has just cleared off a scissor screen movement off No. 4. Now No. 2 and No. 3 do a split move over No. 5. Neither player is open so No. 2 moves on to his left and creates a second split or screen for No. 1 at just about the free throw line. No. 1 has drifted vertically toward the basket and if he

DIAGRAM 2-7

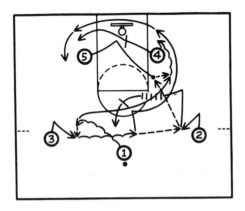

times the move right, he can, in effect, get a double screen move over
No. 2 and No. 5. This should free No. 1 for an easy jump shot or for a
drive to the basket for an easier shot. After furnishing the screen move
for No. 1, No. 2 rolls back out to the outside for defensive floor balance.
If no opening has come from this move, No. 5 has the same option as was
given in Diagrams 2-4 and 2-5. He can look for an opening to pass to No. 3
coming off a screen from behind No. 4 or he can pass the ball back out to
the outside to No. 2 who will look to hit No. 3 on this move. If No. 3
is not open, then No. 4 can break up the lane for the possibility of putting
into play the "pinched-post" move by teaming up with No. 2. This gives
good continuity to the whole offense.

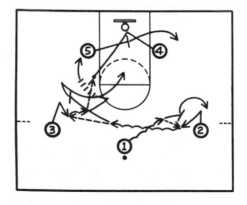

DIAGRAM 2-8

There is another weave pattern that can be used to free the guards
for open breaks and drives for the basket and, at the same time, give an
action that can be synchronized with the movements of No. 4 and No. 5,
the pivot-post men. As in Diagram 2-8, No. 1 moves on a dribble to his
right. No. 2 frees himself in the area and No. 1 passes to No. 2 and moves
inside him to give a screen. No. 2, dribbling off the screen, may go all the
way or force a switch in the defense in which case he could stop and shoot
or possibly catch No. 1 on a roll-off cut to the basket. If this move should
occur, No. 4 and No. 5 must clear the area so as not to jam the drive. In
this diagram, No. 2 dribbles on toward the middle of the floor and passes
to No. 3, and then moves inside him for a screen. Now, as No. 3 starts a

dribble move to his right, he passes into No. 4 on the pivot-post and No. 2 and No. 3 do a "split" action over the pivot-post.

In Diagram 2-9, No. 1 passes the ball to No. 2 and peels off down the middle for a return pass. Not being open, he goes to his right along the baseline. No. 2 dribbles to his right and passes to No. 1 coming up from

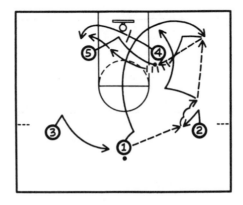

DIAGRAM 2-9

the baseline cut for a pass. In the meantime, No. 5 comes off a screen scissor move around No. 4 and is open in the pivot area. No. 1 passes the ball to No. 5 and No. 1 and No. 2 now do a "split" move over No. 5. If no openings occur from this move, they immediately look for the openings that could come from the Phase 2 continuity on the play (shown in Diagram 2-10).

Diagram 2-10 is a continuation of Diagram 2-9. No. 5 has the ball in the pivot-post area. Nos. 1, 2, and 4 continue to the positions shown. No. 1 and No. 4 are in excellent position for double screening action. No. 2 now cuts along the baseline and cuts out from behind No. 1 and No. 4 for a double screen. No. 5 either passes the ball to him or relays the ball outside to No. 3, who passes to No. 2 as he comes around the double screen. He should have an excellent jump shot from this position or an opportunity to drive in for a layup shot. If no opening has occurred with this action, they immediately go into Phase 3, shown in Diagram 2-11.

In Diagram 2-11 (Phase 3), No. 5 has passed the ball out to No. 3. No. 2, not being open, continues on across the free-throw lane and clears the area. Now No. 1, using No. 4 as a screen, breaks from behind him up to a position in front for a possible jump shot or a drive for the basket. If he is not open, he clears out of the area. Then No. 4 breaks up the lane to a position in the outer half of the free-throw circle and on the left side of the lane to furnish a post screen for a dribble drive by No. 3. No. 3 drives tight by No. 4, bumping his defensive man into him. He looks for the jump shot or a dribbling drive opportunity all the way to the basket.

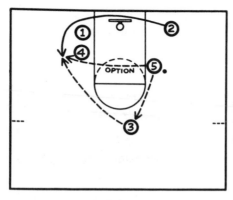

DIAGRAM 2-10

DIAGRAM 2-11

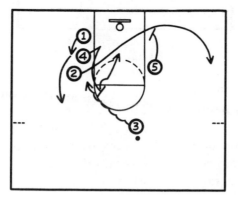

The two pivot-post players may play up and down the lane in the operational pivot-post area. At times the defense may force them to play higher and sometimes the talents of these players may be better suited to a larger range of action and would thus facilitate more scoring opportunities. In Diagram 2-12 they are shown at or just about the free throw line. This position can give the two features in one action, "man ahead of the ball" followed by "ball ahead of the man." No. 1 passes to No. 2 who dribbles to his right in depth and, securing a good passing lane, passes the ball into pivot-post player No. 4. In the meantime, No. 3 who has cut toward the baseline now veers to his right and over the top of pivot-

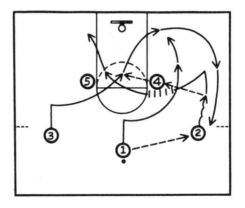

DIAGRAM 2-12

post player No. 5. His timing should be to arrive at the spot in front of No. 5 just as No. 4 receives the ball. No. 4 back bounces the ball to him if he is open. If not open, he clears. Now, immediately following this action, No. 2 and No. 1 do a "split" move over player No. 4. If no opening comes from these moves, the same continuity series can be run from this as was shown in Diagrams 2-9, 2-10, and 2-11, and is given as Phase 2 in Diagram 2-13.

From the previous moves in Diagram 2-12 the team can go into the same continuity moves given in Diagrams 2-10 and 2-11. Diagram 2-13 shows how the moves would be made from the "high" double pivot-post

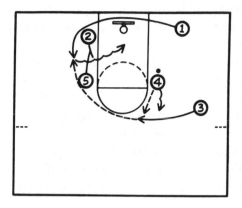

DIAGRAM 2-13

DIAGRAM 2-14

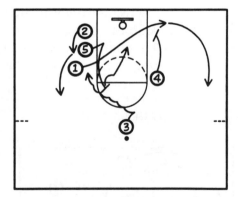

position. No. 4 has the ball. No. 5 now moves down the side of the free throw lane to a position tight with No. 2. No. 1 now breaks across the lane and cuts out from behind No. 2 and No. 5 for a double screen. No. 4 can pass to him or do a dribble-out clear and relay the ball to him, or he can pass the ball outside to No. 3 who has now cleared to the outside. No. 3 can relay the ball into No. 1 who looks for a jump shot or a drive. If no openings occur from this move, then the maneuver continues as given in Diagram 2-14, Phase 3.

With no scoring opportunity presenting itself in the previous moves off this play, No. 1 now clears across the free throw lane and out (see Diagram 2-14). Now No. 2 breaks out from below No. 5 to secure a screen and a possible opening. If he is open, No. 3 or No. 4 passes him the ball for a jump shot or a drive. If he is not open, No. 2 clears and No. 5 breaks up to the left top-side of the free throw circle to furnish a screen for a dribble drive by No. 3 and a possible jump shot or an open drive all the way. If the defense splits on the move and is tight on No. 3's dribble, he looks for an opportunity to pass to No. 5 on a roll-off move, cutting into the basket and a possible additional scoring option.

As has been explained earlier, the two pivot-post men No. 4 and No. 5 may play "tight" in close to the lane or they may play wide in an "open" game. The open game provides more driving opportunities for the outside men and allows the pivot-post men more area in which to maneuver. In Diagram 2-15 No. 1 passes the ball to No. 2 and drives through the open lane area for a clearing move. He in effect has also passed his "trigger" responsibilities to No. 2, who must now make his move. No. 2 moves to the right and passes into No. 5 on the pivot-post position, who has just cleared a screening movement with No. 4 to get open. No. 2 and No. 3 now do a "split" move over No. 5. If no opening occurs, the continuity pattern for double screening moves can now be made or they can clear out, bring the ball outside and setting up the offense again.

DIAGRAM 2-15

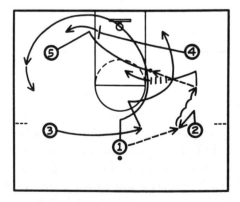

In the open set-up of the pivot-post men, many cutting and driving opportunities present themselves. They can start with the open game and end up with the double screen continuity series that has been previously explained. In Diagram 2-16, No. 1 triggers the offense by dribble driving toward No. 2. This is the signal for No. 2 to clear, and he does so with a drive through the lane. Now, instead of No. 4 doing a scissor screen move with No. 5, he moves out to play with No. 1. No. 1 may pass to No. 4 and cut inside for a screen or a return pass, or he may cut outside for a return pass and a roll-off option to No. 4. He may also dribble outside No. 4 for a screen and possible roll-off motion by No. 4. Phase 3 in Diagram 2-17 will give the continuation of the play.

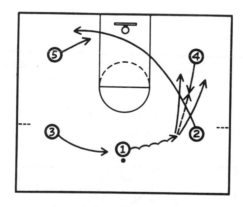

DIAGRAM 2-16

In Diagram 2-17, No. 1 has passed the ball to No. 4. He chose the outside option. No. 4 passed back to No. 1 on the outside move and rolled out toward the basket for a possible opening that might come from a split in the defense on a switch. Not being open, No. 4 continued on to execute a scissor screen move with No. 5 who breaks into the pivot area. No. 1 passes to No. 5 and cuts over the top of him for another possible opening. No. 3 and No. 1 could do a split move over No. 5 but if No. 5 is as low or near the basket as shown here, this is not advisable as it will jam the area near the basket too much and restrict the possible pivot scoring moves that No. 5 could make. If no scoring opportunities present themselves, the double screen continuity moves previously explained could be executed with No. 4 and No. 1 forming the double screen for either No. 3 and No.

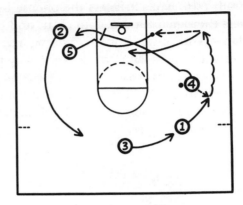

DIAGRAM 2-17

5. No. 5 could relay the ball back out to No. 2 who could trigger the continued series as either No. 3 or No. 5 come along the baseline and up behind the double screen.

DIAGRAM 2-18

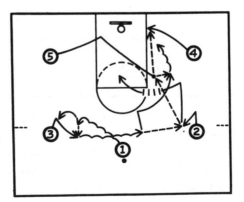

In the open or wide positions of play, the pivot-post men can frequently "flash" the pivot area with success (see Diagram 2-18). When this happens, the teammate pivot-post player can cut the baseline with success at times, and another option much like the "Sucker Play." Here No. 1 starts the move to the left and hands off to No. 3, who moves the ball toward the middle and passes off to No. 2. No. 2 relays the ball into No. 5 who has flashed the pivot area from the weak side. No. 5's first look should be for his teammate No. 4 who cuts the baseline. If open, he passes him the ball. If this option is not available, then he has the options that will come from the "split" move over the post by players No. 3 and No. 2.

3

The Weak-Side Cutter Series

(Reverse Action Offense)

The offense presented in this chapter and herein called the Weak-Side Cutter Series is one that has been used by many famous and successful teams. It has well earned the status of being one of the "Ten Great Basketball Offenses." It could be seen in action on a given basketball night in any part of the United States. It might be observed in use in a high school game, a college or university contest, and even on the pro circuits. It has been alluded to by many names, one of the more prevalent being the "Reverse Action Offense."

In reality the Weak-Side Cutter Series is a re-deployment of the pivot-post offense, with the three players nearest the basket interchanging positions in a movement by, over, or around the player in the pivot-post area to secure openings. This features a player, or players, always moving from the courtside away from the ball toward the ball. The "weak side" always refers to the side of the court away from the ball, while the "strong side" is always regarded as the side where the ball is in possession by a player.

The popularity of this offense did not come about without good reason. It has all the factors that are needed for a championship offense. It has continuity of movement and pattern and can be run continuously from side to side until a scoring opportunity presents itself. It can have as much variety and as many options as the coach wants to add. These variations can be added or altered to secure the full potential of the talent in the players available. The offense can be used in a deliberate way and it can also be very explosive, with surprise being a possibility at any time. No defense dare nap during this attack.

No particular player requirements are needed for the various positions in the offense. The talents of the players could run about the same as those given in the Single Pivot-Post, the Double Pivot-Post, or most any other offense given in this book. It is a two-out and three-in offense, meaning by this that two guards bring the ball down the floor and the other three players play nearer the basket, with one of them being stationed somewhere in the pivot-post area. Thereafter, these three have a movement that will bring about an interchange of positions that can be continuous and that will result in scoring opportunities.

Two movements to the Weak-Side Cutter Series will be given here. The first is a *guard outside* option move. In this option the guard moves to the baseline by going outside the forward position and then to the baseline. The other option—the *guard inside* move, in which the guard moves inside the forward to the baseline and out again, or options to move in for a scissor screening play with the pivot player and the opposite forward—does not present quite as much continuity of movement, but has explosive possibilities.

Diagram 3-1 illustrates the basic two-out and three-in offensive formation. This shows the formation for the movement of the ball to the right side. The attack should be balanced and go to the left side as often as to the right side, but one of the features of the guard-outside option to this offense is that it swings from one side to the other in a continuous reverse

DIAGRAM 3-1

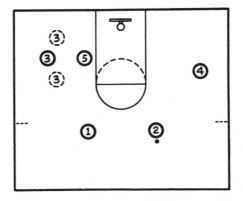

action movement which always has a player breaking or cutting from the weak side to the strong side for scoring opportunities. The center or the pivot-post player will start anywhere along the free throw lane. He can be high or low, but should be so stationed as to furnish a good screen for No. 3 as he cuts by, over, or around him. The forwards, Nos. 3 and 4, station themselves as shown, with No. 4 nearer the sideline and back of the free throw line extended. No. 3's position is a key position. He may need to vary his position as shown since he will need to make his move by No. 5 in such a manner as to secure a screen on No. 5. The guards, Nos. 1 and 2, are spread about the width of the free throw lane and may vary this up to about 15 feet. The guards will always start the offense to the side opposite the free throw lane from No. 5, or the player in this position. Later diagrams will show how the player in this position is not always No. 5, but will be a constant interchange, with numbers 3, 4, and 5 playing the position.

Phase 1 is the first move of the Weak-Side Cutter Series (see Diagram 3-2). The first six phases of the play will present the complete turnover of the players, with the play having been run from side to side and each of the players returning to their original positions, as given here in Phase 1. While making this complete turnover, many scoring opportunities could develop. In the first move shown here, No. 2 starts the offense by passing the ball into No. 4 and following the pass going outside and on to a position near the baseline. As the ball is passed to No. 4, No. 3 starts a jockeying movement to cut by No. 5 for a screen. It is his job to run his defensive man into No. 5 so as to secure an opening for a pass from No. 4.

DIAGRAM 3-2

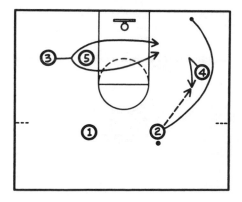

No. 5 is not to be concerned with this except to remain in his position so that No. 3 may jockey his position and bump his defensive man into No. 5. No. 5 should face the action where the ball is and may even have his back to No. 3. No. 3 cuts either over, around, or behind No. 5. In the majority of the situations, No. 3 will find it to the best advantage to do the low cut behind No. 5. However, he must learn to vary this move, to mix them up so that the offense can be more explosive and present more scoring opportunities. The low and high cut options are shown in the diagram and No. 3 arrives at the spot shown. Diagram 3-3 will show the next moves to be made from these positions to achieve continuity.

In Diagram 3-3 (Phase 2), the players have arrived at the positions shown here through the moves given in Phase 1, Diagram 3-2. If no scoring opportunities have occurred, No. 4 passes the ball back out to No. 1, who has adjusted his position to balance the action. No. 2 now leaves the baseline and comes back to the outside. No. 1 quickly moves the ball to the left side of the floor and No. 5 breaks out from the pivot-post area to the forward position on the left side. No. 1 passes the ball to No. 5 and breaks outside and to the baseline spot. While this is being done, No. 3 adjusts his position in the pivot-post area so that No. 4, with slight adjustments of position, can cut by him to secure a screen as he bumps his defensive man into No. 3 in the same kind of move as was made between No. 3 and No. 5 in Phase 1. Several possibilities for scoring are present here as No. 4 breaks around No. 3: No. 4 may be open, No. 3 may cut up for openings off defensive switches. By no means should the offense ever neglect the guard on the baseline. If his defensive player sluffs off, he should be passed

DIAGRAM 3-3

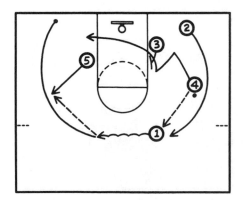

the ball for the shot that he could obtain from here. If the guards are good shots from along the baseline, it helps to keep the defense honest against this offense and makes it more effective.

In Diagram 3-4 (Phase 3), the players are now in position, with No. 5 in possession of the ball. No. 2, who has returned from the baseline position reached on his first cut, adjusts his outside position. Another important factor in this offense is for Nos. 1 and 2 to be good enough middle distance shooters that the defense cannot sag or sluff off on these players. If they do sag off, the defense can more effectively jam the middle offensive moves. If the defense sags off and the teammates pass the ball to the guards for effective scoring shots, the defense will have to stay honest on these two players. No. 5, with the ball, had the possible options of passing to No. 4, No. 3, or No. 1. None of these being possible, he now passes the ball back out to No. 2. Now the action reverses again, with No. 2 taking the ball to the right side and quickly passing into No. 3 who moves out to the forward position. No. 1 reverses back out to the outside, and No. 4 and No. 5 quickly position themselves for No. 5 to break from the weak side toward the ball, cutting over, by, or around No. 4 to secure a screen.

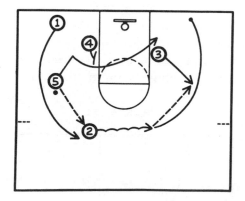

DIAGRAM 3-4

In Diagram 3-5 (Phase 4), the players have now arrived in the positions shown. No. 3 has the ball and again the reverse action takes place with No. 3 passing the ball to No. 1. No. 1 passes to No. 4 who has quickly come out to the forward position. No. 1 cuts to the baseline on the left side and No. 3 becomes the weak side cutter, moving by No. 5 in attempt-

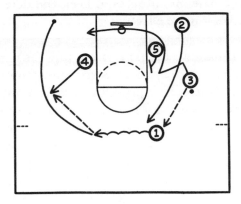

DIAGRAM 3-5

ing to bump his defensive man off in a screen. The reverse action again brings about an interchange of positions with Nos. 3, 4, and 5. No. 3 will now be in the pivot position, and No. 4 and No. 5 will be in the forward positions. As Diagrams 3-6 and 3-7 will show, when they have done six movements, all players will be back at their original positions, on the same side of the floor from which they started in Phase 1.

In Diagram 3-6 (Phase 5), No. 4 has the ball, passes it out to No. 2 who again reverses it to the right side and repeats his cut outside of No. 5 to the baseline. No. 4, now the weak side cutter, moves over No. 3 and the players arrive at the positions shown in Diagram 3-7.

DIAGRAM 3-6

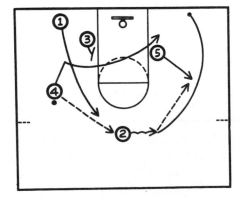

In Diagram 3-7 (Phase 6), the reverse action again takes place with No. 5 being the weak side cutter. The players have now made six moves on the reverse action movement, with weak side cutters constantly breaking in toward the ball. Many scoring opportunities could have been available during this time. After this sixth move, with No. 3 returning the ball outside to No. 2, and No. 1 returning to the outside, the players would be in their original starting positions (see Diagram 3-8) and players No. 3, 4, and 5 would have rotated in the pivot and forward positions, each having been in each position on both sides of the floor.

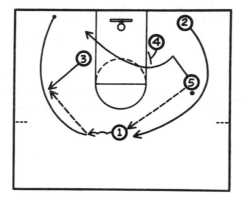

DIAGRAM 3-7

DIAGRAM 3-8

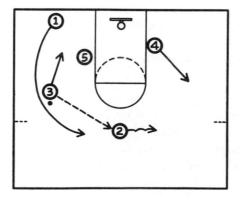

When No. 3 passes the ball back outside to No. 2, as shown in Diagram 3-8, and No. 1 returns to the outside, the players are back in their beginning positions, having completely turned the offense over once in six moves from side to side, with Nos. 3, 4, and 5 each having been in each position once on each side of the floor. They are now back, ready to turn the offense over again, if necessary, to secure scoring opportunities.

POSSIBILITIES AND OPTIONS TO THE OFFENSE

This offense has many possibilities and can give surprise scoring punches. As shown in the first eight diagrams, it can give good scoring options in close to the basket. As players No. 3, 4, and 5 alternate positions and take their breaks in toward the center of the floor and to the basket, they can take advantage of any mistakes that the defense makes.

The success of the offense and the movements to a large extent will depend upon how well the weak side forward sets his defensive man up for a screen as he cuts by the teammate in the pivot-post position. By faking, jockeying his position, etc., it is up to this weak side cutter to get a commitment from the defensive player guarding him. Once he gets this commitment, he then cuts over the top or low behind the pivot man to get the best screening or bumping action possible according to the play of the defensive man. It is to the advantage of the offense for the weak side cutter to take the low cut behind the pivot-post man whenever possible, for this move will place the cutter closer to the basket and in a higher percentage scoring area.

Remember also that there are two movements to the weak side cutter series, (1) the guard outside option, and (2) the guard inside option. The weak side cutter should always hold his move by the pivot-post player until the guard has made his commitment to either the outside move to the baseline or the inside move which is more to the middle. If he does not do this, he may find the middle jammed, arriving there at the same time as the guard should he choose the guard inside move. But, while the guard is making this commitment, the weak side player can be very busy maneuvering his defensive player into position so that when he does make his cut, he can secure an effective screen as he breaks by the pivot-post.

In reality this shuttle move of reverse action from side to side seems very simple and at first the impression is that the weak side cutter move is so simple that surely no one could get by with it. Yet, year after year teams have used this simple move with increasing success by working options that take advantage of defensive mistakes or switches. Some of the possibilities are given in the diagrams that follow.

The very simplest part of the movement is given in Diagram 3-9. No. 2 has passed the ball to No. 4 and made his cut to the baseline. No. 3, the weak side cutter, fakes behind No. 5, got a commitment from his defensive man, and cut over the top of the pivot-post position, which in this case is No. 5. If the defense does not switch, then surely No. 3 will be open for a pass from No. 4 and an easy scoring opportunity. No. 3 could just as well have faked a cut over the top of No. 5 and cut behind him for the same kind of opening, one that might be preferred in the majority of cases since it would place him closer to the basket. If the defense does switch, the switch would have to be almost perfect in its execution to prevent No. 3 from being eligible for receipt of a pass. Even if the switch is successful, other possibilities are open to No. 3 and No. 5 as will be shown later. In this maneuver No. 3 should be taught to run his defensive man into the screen that is set by the pivot-post player. The pivot-post player is not to perform the act of screening and should never turn his back to the ball.

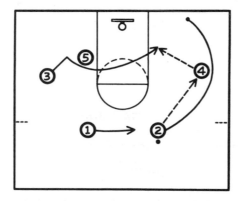

DIAGRAM 3-9

If the defense does switch, as shown in Diagram 3-10, some possibilities present themselves from this simple move. No. 2 has passed into No. 4 and again taken the outside move to the baseline. No. 3 fakes to drive low behind No. 5 and getting X3 in position, cuts over the top of No. 5. Defensive player X5 switches to No. 3 to prevent a pass to him and a scoring opportunity. No. 5, however, at least for an instant, will have X3 on his hip in the screening movement or he may see the move coming and pivot so as to catch X3 on his hip to get him out of the play for an instant. As soon as the switch is made No. 3 moves up higher and No. 5

cuts in deep ahead of X3 for a fine opening right next to the basket. Another point that it is important to stress on this move is to be sure the weak side cutter, No. 3 in this case, does not make his cut too soon. If he makes his move before No. 4 can pass to him or before No. 2 has made a commitment, then no scoring opportunity can occur at all. If he makes his move late, there can still be scoring opportunities. It is better to have the timing of the cut perfect, but if an error in timing is to be made, it is better to err on the side of being too late on the cut than to be too soon in making the cut.

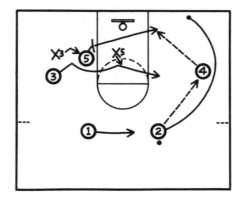

DIAGRAM 3-10

DIAGRAM 3-11

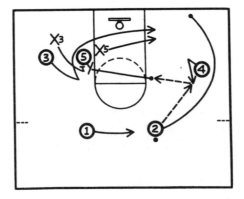

In Diagram 3-11, No. 3, the weak side cutter, fakes a move over the top of No. 5, the pivot-post player. Getting a commitment from the defensive player X3, No. 3 reverses his move to cut behind No. 5 and catch X3 on No. 5's hip for a screen. X5, the defensive player guarding No. 5, switches to No. 3 to prevent him from receiving a pass from No. 4 and having an easy two points. Now, at an instant of the defensive switch, X3 is on No. 5's hip and, since No. 3 has cut low, No. 5 breaks out higher to receive the pass from No. 4. He could be open for a good shot from here or take advantage of other opportunities. One of the opportunities that can come from defensive switches is that a short defensive man may switch to a taller offensive player. In this case, the difference in height could be exploited by either No. 3 or No. 5.

A few of the many possibilities from the offense will now be given. In Diagram 3-12 the guard No. 2 passes to No. 4 and goes outside to the baseline. No. 3, the weak side cutter, moves across behind No. 5 and is not open. No. 5 now moves up the free throw lane toward the top of the circle. No. 4 passes to him if he is open. No. 5 may shoot a jump shot, drive, or he may hand off to No. 1 cutting by on a pinched-post move. If No. 5 is not open, No. 4 can pass the ball out to No. 1, who can pass the ball to No. 5 and cut back off him for a hand off and a drive for the basket or a jump shot. The possible pass from No. 4 to No. 5 may look like a long cross-court pass, but in this situation there is little likelihood of interception because the defense is likely to be sagging from the quick move that No. 3 made by No. 5. If No. 5 moves quickly to the position shown, he will be open here for many easy jump shots. If he is not open, the pinched-post maneuver can be quickly executed.

DIAGRAM 3-12

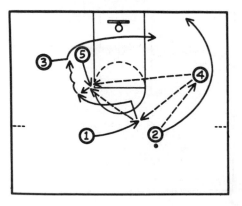

In Diagram 3-13, No. 1 passes the ball to No. 2. No. 2 relays the ball on to No. 4 and cuts outside. As No. 2 cuts outside, No. 4 hands or passes the ball back to No. 2, who now dribbles the ball down toward the baseline and then passes the ball back to No. 4. No. 3, the weak side cutter, has maneuvered in behind No. 5, the pivot-post player, and is open for a pass from No. 4. This pass could have come from No. 2 if No. 3 had arrived at this point open before No. 2 passed the ball back to No. 4. After passing the ball into No. 3, No. 4 and No. 2 cut by No. 3 as shown and either may receive a pass from No. 3 for a short jump shot or other moves that will secure a scoring opportunity for them.

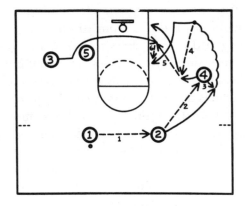

DIAGRAM 3-13

DIAGRAM 3-14

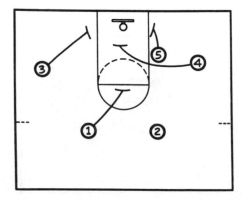

Rebound responsibilities should always be set and definite. The players will need much drill on this and some variations will be necessary in the different plays, when shots are taken from the different positions on the floor. Generally speaking though, the rebounding responsibilities will be as shown in Diagram 3-14, with the player on the pivot-post going in on his side. As shown, the player on the side with the pivot-post player crashes for the middle while the player on the opposite side covers that side. One of the guards will take responsibility for the long rebound in the free throw area. If these principles are followed, rebounding should be definite and effective.

The double pick option, Phase 1, is shown in Diagram 3-15. Many double pick options for either the guards or the forwards can be worked from this offense. This one is a double pick for the forward who begins as the weak side cutter. No. 2 passes the ball to No. 4 and cuts outside to the baseline. No. 3 fakes his defensive man into a commitment behind No. 5 and cuts over the top of him. With no opening, No. 4 quickly passes the ball back out to No. 1, who now passes the ball to No. 5 who has come out to the forward position on the left side of the floor. No. 1 cuts outside No. 5 to the baseline and No. 2, as soon as No. 4 passes the ball back out to No. 1, retraces his move to the baseline back out to the outside again. Diagram 3-16, Phase 2, will give the play from here.

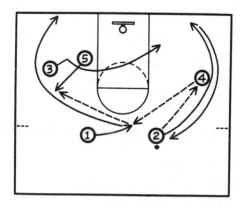

DIAGRAM 3-15

After the completion of Phase 1, Diagram 3-15, the players have arrived at the positions shown in Diagram 3-16. At a pre-given signal, when this point is reached, it is understood that the double pick play is on. No. 5

passes the ball back out to No. 2. No. 2 starts the ball to the right side as is usually done on the reverse action from side to side. Instead of passing in, he dribbles as shown and works an exchange with No. 4, who comes out to take a hand-off from No. 2. As soon as No. 5 has passed to No. 2, he moves in along the free throw lane with No. 1 in a shoulder-to-shoulder position to form a double screen for No. 3, who cuts across the free throw lane and in behind No. 1 and No. 5 to get the full effect of the double screen in brushing his defensive man off. No. 4, who dribbled to the middle of the floor after receiving the hand-off from No. 2, passes the ball into No. 3. No. 3 can take a short jump shot, but if the defense thwarts this effort, he can drive for the basket or possibly pass off to No. 1 or No. 5 who may be open in the defensive shuffle. If none of these options are available, he can still pass the ball back out to No. 4 or No. 2.

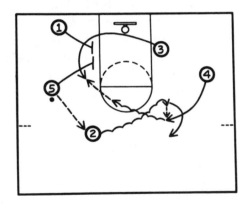

DIAGRAM 3-16

This series would not be complete without a double pick for the guards as well as the forwards. This move actually combines three possibilities all into one. They are (1) the sucker play, (2) the pinched post move, and (3) the double pick for the guard. This play can be triggered anywhere along the way in the reverse action movement of the Weak Side Cutter Series. The ball has arrived at the point shown in Diagram 3-17 and, instead of taking the ball to the side of the floor away from the pivot-post man, No. 2 passes to No. 1 and No. 1 starts a dribble move to his left toward the side of No. 3 and No. 5. Now No. 2 drifts to his right and No. 4 jabs toward the baseline and quickly breaks to his left to the top of the free throw circle. No. 1 passes him the ball. From here several options are possible. As No. 2 breaks in as shown, if his defensive man has turned his eye to watch the ball, he could be wide open on a "sucker" play. If so, No. 4 passes him the ball. If not open, he continues on as shown, and No. 3 and No. 5 move in along the free throw line, in a shoulder-to-shoulder position so that, as No. 2 continues on across the free throw lane, he can break in behind No. 3 and No. 5 for a double pick. No. 4 can pass to No. 2 as he comes in behind No. 3 and No. 5, where he can take an easy jump shot; or if this option is cut off, he may drive or pass off to No. 3 or No. 5 if defensive shifts have left either of them open. Another option that can be used on this play in effect is the pinched-post play, which could be brought in with No. 1 following his pass to No. 4 and breaking tight over the top for a return pass here from No. 4 and a possible jump shot or a drive for the basket.

THE GUARD INSIDE OPTION

The guard inside option brings up several possibilities and is put in the offense for the purpose of keeping the defense honest. The guard inside option can also take on two moves or options, and it can be run as a continuity series, reversing from side to side in a continuous movement, or it may be cut short, run as one option with the offense reforming again if the first scoring opportunity fails. All of these possibilities will be explained in the ensuing diagrams.

After running the guard outside option a few times the defensive players guarding the guards may soon get the idea that the guards, No. 1 and No. 2, after passing the ball inside, always cut to the outside. Their next move to combat this is to overshift the guards and to make their move to the outside more difficult. When this happens, the guard inside option should be taken. In its simplest form, after passing the ball to the forward on the side, the guard could cut straight down the middle for a return pass from the forward and a simple scoring opportunity or a possible clearing move. If this simple scoring play does not result, then it is up to the guard to trigger one of the two possible options left. The first is the *forward scissor,* and the second is the *diagonal play.* The guard triggers the play by his cut and move. These two plays, with possible options, will be explained in the following diagrams.

The Forward Scissor

The forward scissor fits right in a perfect pattern with the Weak Side Cutter Series in that it features players cutting from the weak side of the court to the middle and toward the ball for openings. It can be more explosive in that it affords opportunities for a double screen on every move, with several possibilities—enough options to make it a guessing game for the defense. If the offense will use a little imagination and ingenuity the defense may soon acquire the idea that regardless of how they switch or move, the offense will have a possibility for a quick opening some way.

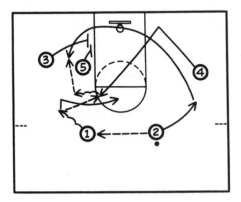

DIAGRAM 3-17

The simplest move and first possibility from the guard inside move is shown in Diagram 3-18. No. 2 passes the ball to No. 4, and with the defensive man overshifting, No. 2 drives straight down the middle. If he

DIAGRAM 3-18

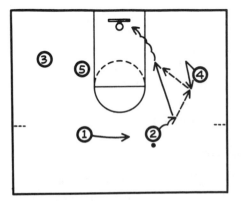

is open, No. 4 passes him the ball with a lead bounce pass being the best possibility. If he is not open, then No. 2 will continue on into the options shown in the following diagrams.

If on the simple break-away given in Diagram 3-18, No. 2 is not open, then he may elect to go into the forward scissor move or he may go into the diagonal play. In Diagram 3-19 he triggers the forward scissor by continuing on and then fading to his right and then in behind No. 4 near the baseline. No. 4 may turn and drop the ball to No. 2, or he may fire it out to No. 1, who may then relay it into No. 2 on his way out from the baseline. As soon as No. 4 passes the ball off, he cuts in a move across the free throw lane so as to arrive in a position near No. 5, just as No. 3, who has jockeyed his defensive man into position, breaks over or around No. 5. No. 4's arriving here will create, in effect, a double screen or pick for No. 3 as he goes by. No. 4 and No. 5 can maneuver their positions to make this possible. After No. 3 cuts by, No. 5 will then break out toward the ball for openings. If No. 3 cuts low, No. 5 will cut high. If No. 3 should cut high, No. 5 will cut low. Several possible openings can come from these moves. Diagram 3-20, Phase 2, will give the next continuity move from the pattern.

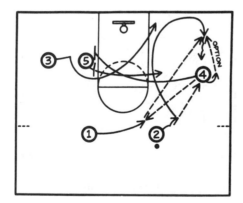

DIAGRAM 3-19

In Phase 2 of the forward scissor (Diagram 3-20), the players have now arrived in the positions shown. No. 2 can shuttle the ball up and down the sideline area to get a good passing angle on No. 3 and No. 5 as they break across. If no openings, now the ball is sent into reverse action to take the move to the opposite side of the floor. No. 2 passes the ball out to No. 1 who quickly moves to his left and then passes into No. 4 who has moved out to the forward position after his scissor and double screening move on the previous play. No. 1 cuts down the middle and then in behind No. 4.. No. 4 now either passes the ball to No. 1 in behind him or relays it out to No. 2, who passes into No. 1. After passing off, No. 4 again starts a move across the free throw lane and repeats the double screening or pick all over again with No. 3 and No. 5. At the completion of the two moves, the players would be back in their original positions if the players are deployed in the manner shown here in Phases 1 and 2. In other words, when Phase 2 is completed and the ball is passed outside again and No. 1 returns to the outside, all players will be back in the positions relative to where they started in Phase 1. Note that No. 4 is the player that makes all the cross-court scissor moves in this play. If the play had been started to the opposite side, then No. 3 would be making these moves on the swing back and forth. As shown here, No. 5 keeps his pivot-post position in the moves back and forth. It is easy to change No. 3 and No. 5 by just breaking No. 5 first in one of the moves and adjusting positions accordingly.

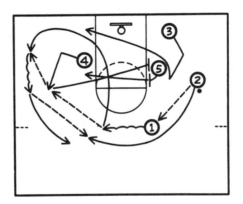

DIAGRAM 3-20

Some scoring opportunities in the forward scissor play other than the ones already shown will now be given. As shown in Diagram 3-21, at a given signal No. 3 and No. 5 can change their cuts for not only a change in positions but a quick explosive move that could confuse the defense. The play has started as usual. No. 2 passing to No. 4 cuts down the middle and then in behind No. 4. No. 4 drops the ball down to No. 2 or whips it out to No. 1 who relays it back to No. 2. No. 4 moves across the lane to screen for No. 3 and No. 5. No. 3 starts his cut over the top of No. 5 and No. 4, but just as he gets about even with No. 5, No. 3 stops short. No. 5 either breaks over or under No. 4, faking his defensive man one way, breaking the other. Actually the defensive man will decide his cut. Most of the time a low cut near the basket is best and No. 2 can pass to him if he is open. After No. 5 cuts, No. 3 now fakes his defensive man and cuts by No. 4. The defense will call his move also and he will break to a position according to the defensive shuffle on this play.

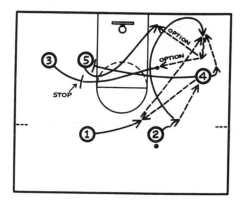

DIAGRAM 3-21

Diagram 3-22 carries out the idea a little farther and is not complicated, even though it looks that way. It actually combines the forward scissor with the guard diagonal move that will be explained next. The

DIAGRAM 3-22

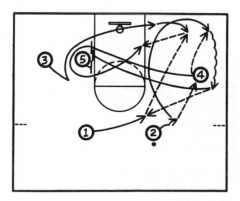

forward goes into the scissor move, the center holds his position, and the guard shuttles the ball out and goes into the scissor move that we refer to as the diagonal play in the Weak Side Cutter Series. Here No. 2 passes to No. 4 and cuts down the middle and in behind No. 4. No. 4 drops the ball to him and scissors in with No. 5 to form a double screen for No. 3 cutting by. Now No. 5 holds his position and No. 2 shuttles the ball up the sideline and passes it to No. 1 who passes it to No. 3. No. 3, after breaking across the lane, had dropped in behind No. 2. Now, after passing the ball, No. 2 cuts across the free throw lane and forms a double screen for No. 4 who has adjusted his position so as to break out of the area toward the ball, but around, over or behind No. 2 and No. 5. No. 3 passes to him if he is open. No. 5 and No. 2 could also break out of this pattern for openings that present themselves. The options are unlimited.

Diagram 3-23 begins the explanation of the diagonal play. It has sometimes been called the "guard scissor play" or "option." The guard triggers this play just as he does the others and remember this is an option to the guard inside move off the Weak Side Cutter Series. No. 2 passes in to No. 4 and starts his move to the middle and inside. Not being open, this time, instead of continuing on through and in behind No. 4, he cuts in a diagonal direction so as to go into a scissor move, forming a double screen for No. 3 as he makes his move to the middle toward the ball. No. 3 breaks over No. 5 and No. 2. After No. 3 cuts by, No. 5 moves out for a possible opening also. No. 3 and No. 5 have all the possible openings and change movements that they had off the forward scissor. Diagram 3-24 will give the next continuity move.

DIAGRAM 3-23

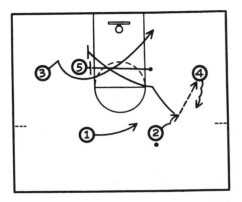

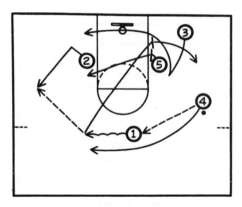

DIAGRAM 3-24

The players through Phase 1 have arrived in the positions shown in Diagram 3-24. Now we get the reverse action again and the swing back to the opposite side. Here we get a difference—the guard, No. 2, now moves into one of the forward positions for a moment and No. 4 moves out to the guard position until the next swing back. No. 5 holds his position or he may work a change with No. 3 on a switch move. If this play had started to the left, then No. 1 and No. 3 would be in the guard-forward switch moves. After six continuity moves or phases, the players would all be back to their original positions. At the completion of phase 1, No. 4 had the ball. He now passing it out to No. 1. No. 1, reversing the play, moves to his left and passes into No. 2 who, moving off the diagonal cut, now comes out to the forward position to receive the ball. After passing to No. 2, No. 1 starts down the middle and then goes diagonally across the lane so as to help No. 5 form a double screen for No. 3 cutting by. Then No. 5 cuts out to the position shown.

At the completion of Phase 2 the players were as shown in Diagram 3-25. Now No. 2 passes the ball out to No. 4 and comes back out to the outside. No. 4 passes into No. 1 and goes on the diagonal cut across the lane to form the double screen for No. 3 and No. 5. Actually, the diagonal move from the Weak Side Cutter Series has players No. 1, 2, and 4 rotating in the guard position and in making diagonal cuts to form double pick and screens for players No. 3 and No. 5. If the play should start to the left, it would have players No. 1, 2, and 3 rotating at guard and making the diagonal moves for Nos. 4 and 5. At the completion of six moves the players will have turned the continuity pattern over once and they will be back in the original starting positions. It will not be necessary to here show all these as the first three phases clearly give the moves and show how the continuity pattern of the diagonal move would work.

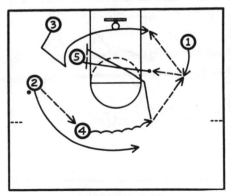

DIAGRAM 3-25

Many quick and explosive moves are possible off the diagonal move. Diagram 3-26 gives one such move. Here No. 2 passes into No. 4. Then, after starting a move toward the middle, he cuts in on the diagonal option and takes a position shoulder to shoulder with No. 5 along the free throw lane. No. 3 cuts by them toward the ball, but after getting by them, reverses and comes back behind the double pick. No. 4 passed the ball quickly to No. 1 and No. 1 maneuvered to get the timing and passed the ball to No. 3 just as he reversed direction and came in behind the screen. A quick jump shot should be possible from here, but if not, then he could use No. 2 and No. 5 as posts from around which he could dribble and drive for the basket.

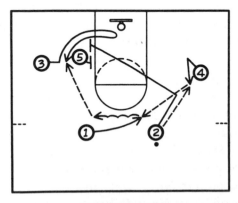

DIAGRAM 3-26

Your imagination can take you anywhere with the Weak-Side Cutter Series—it can give you as much variation as the talent of your players will absorb.

4

The 1-3-1 Offense

(The Hi-Lo Offense)

This offense has been designated by many names. One famous coach called it the "Vertical-Pivot Offense" and referred to the pivot men as vertical pivots. Another coach referred to the offense as the "Tandum Pivot-Post Offense," and still another called it the "Hi-Lo Offense." Regardless of the name, the game is the same!

The 1-3-1 offense gets its name from the manner in which the players are positioned or deployed on the floor in the offense. It actually is a Double Pivot-Post offense and could be called such, but certainly it is not the same operation or deployment and use of players as is made in most Double Pivot-Post offenses.

When and where the offense originated no one seems to be certain, but by the middle 1950's the offense was in wide usage. It is still a very popular offense and widely used in many variations and patterns. The 1-3-1 formation has been adapted in some manner to nearly all the other offenses and one of the most popular offenses now adapted to this formation is the Shuffle offense. The 1-3-1 offense may have come into usage to combat the 1-3-1 zone defense that was popular in the late 1940's and early 1950's. Being used to combat this nuisance, it was soon found that with slight variations in movements, this formation could be used to combat either the man-to-man or the zone and any variation in either.

The offense fits well with the present-day trend in basketball to isolate play so that most situations will be a one-on-one play or at the most, a two-on-two situation. The 1-3-1 spreads the defense in such a manner that sooner or later the one-on-one situation will arise. The offense is deployed so that the defense covering the weak side offensive players must never relax or they will give away good scoring opportunities.

ADVANTAGES OF THE 1-3-1 OFFENSE

The 1-3-1 offense has several advantages and strong points.

1. The offense can be used with slight variations against both zone and man-to-man defenses. This simplifies teaching by necessitating only one formation. (Chapter 10, "The Zone Offense," which features a continuity offense for use against zones, is a 1-3-1 formation.)
2. The offense spreads the defense and makes for many isolation plays of one-on-one or two-on-two.
3. It is easily adaptable to the talent of the players available.
4. In this offense one guard brings the ball down the floor and many coaches claim this is an advantage because with one good quarterback type player bringing the ball down the floor they have fewer interceptions than when two and three guards bring the ball down.
5. It is very advantageous to use this formation against pressing defenses, either full-court or half-court.
6. It can be used equally as well against man-to-man defensive presses and zone defensive presses.
7. It can be used as a free-lance offense or as a disciplined team offense.

DISADVANTAGES OF THE 1-3-1 OFFENSE

1. It is weak in protecting against the fast break. With only one player back in the guard position, extra precautions must be made or the defense will be extremely weak in defending against the fast break.
2. With only one player operating along the baseline area, it has a tendency to be weak in offensive rebounding coverage. (Emphasis and stress on proper player coverage can overcome this weakness.)
3. It requires one exceptionally fine ballhandler and quarterback type player in order for the offense to be really effective. Not every team is fortunate enough to have one such player.
4. In order to be 100% effective, it requires well-balanced personnel with no one player being weak.

BASICS OF THE 1-3-1 OFFENSE

This offense is one of *movement*. Each player must know how to move, where to move, and when to make his cuts. This can best be done by establishing rules or principles for movement for each player in given situations. This offense is not a roll and screen offense—it is a "move the ball—cut and go" offense. The weak side players (offensive players on the side away from the ball) must move. If they do not move, the defense will sag off, gang up, and jam the offense. So one of the first principles to remember in this offense is to move and to use the weak side players.

The offense should always look for, and be alert for, the full and the half-court presses. It is especially well adapted to combat these two defensive devices, and most offenses that successfully penetrate either of these two presses usually takes some expanded form of the 1-3-1 offense.

The 1-3-1 features the open game with free-lance opportunities. With this open, one-on-one situation being the object, one player at a time breaks or cuts. Two cutters on the same movement are to be avoided since this would cause congestion and jamming of the lanes. The offense is built to spread the defense, to prevent congestion and milling around, and to get the one-on-one attack.

If the defense is tight and pressing, the offense will spread, bringing the pivot men farther apart to cope with the spread. If the defense is jammed, then the offense just operates closer together, with the high post and low post operating in closer confines. In actuality the 1-3-1 offense is also a very fine "delayed offense" and can be used to spread the defense in situations where the offensive team can dictate this condition to the defense.

To begin the offense players Nos. 2, 3, 4, and 5 go down the floor and set up in their operational areas, as shown in Diagram 4-1. No. 1, the guard, will bring the ball down the floor, getting help as he needs it from No. 2 first, and possible from Nos. 3, 4, and 5 if needed. However, it is No. 1 who is the quarterback and who triggers most plays starting the offense. He is sometimes called the "point" man. No. 2 and No. 3 are called the "wingmen," but note that No. 2's position is shallow compared to No. 3's position. He plays shallow so as to be able to render aid to No. 1 at anytime he needs it. No. 4 and No. 5 are the pivot men. The players begin their operations in the areas shown. Here the offense is set up to move the offense to the right side. The offense should move to the left as often as to the right, and any operations or plays shown moving to the right will not be duplicated in showing movements to the left. However, it must be remembered that any play going to one side can also be worked from the opposite side.

If the offense should move to the left side, No. 2 and No. 3 could change sides of the floor, with No. 5 taking the opposite side of the lane and No. 3 changing his operational area to the left side and No. 2 taking the shallow position on the right side of the floor. Or, if No. 1 should move the offense to the left, No. 2 could move into the forward operational area on the left side of the floor and No. 3 can move out to the shallow wing position on the right side if these two players have the ability to do an interchange of positions.

In Diagram 4-1, No. 1 is shown taking a position so that the distance between No. 4 and No. 3 is split. With this position split between No. 3 and No. 4, No. 1 has a good passing angle to either No. 4 or No. 3. He may vary this position as needed, and may take a position straight off from No. 4 or one more nearly straight off from No. 3. However, in taking a position straight off from No. 4, his passing angle to No. 4 is poor, and his possibilities of cutting and moving in play situations with No. 3 are poorer. His only advantage in bringing the ball down and lining straight up off No. 4 is that he could balance his moves to the right or left easier from this position.

DIAGRAM 4-1

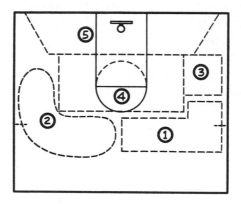

REQUIREMENTS FOR THE PLAYER POSITIONS IN THE 1-3-1 OFFENSE

The requirements for the player positions in this offense will differ somewhat from other offenses and will be given now.

Player No. 1

1. He should be the best ballhandler and the quarterback type of player.
2. He should have speed, quickness, and be able to drive.
3. If he is tall it will help his feeding and passing ability.
4. He should be a good shot 18 to 25 feet away from the basket.
5. He must have defensive ability and sense. He is the first line of defense and must assume this responsibility also.

Player No. 2

1. He must be the combination guard-forward type player.
2. He is the first relief man for No. 1 and takes his position anytime he drives or leaves the position.
3. He actually should be able to operate in No. 3's position or No. 1's position at anytime.
4. He should be an excellent shot from his operational area. The first rule of thumb is: Anytime the player in No. 4's position receives the ball, his first move is to look to see if No. 2 is open and to feed him the ball if he is.
5. He should be able to drive.
6. He should have a keen sense of defensive balance and ability and know when to assist, help, and cover for No. 1 in defensive work.

Player No. 3

1. He should be the typical forward type. It is a rule in this offense that he play on the side of the floor opposite the lane from No. 5.
2. He should be a good shot from his operational area.
3. He should be able to move and drive.
4. He should be a good rebounder and crash the boards for rebounds anytime the shot goes up.

Player No. 4

1. He should be the most active of the two pivot players. Although No. 4 and No. 5 constantly change positions in scissor moves, No. 4 should be the most active big player in the offense. He should be found in the high post position most of the time.
2. He should be a good ballhandler with ability to feed cutting teammates. He should even have the ability to step out and replace No. 1 at times as required.
3. He should be a good shot from the top of the free throw circle and in to the basket.
4. He should be a rugged, aggressive rebounder.
5. He should have a good repertoire of pivot shots and pivot-post moves.

Player No. 5

1. The largest player should play this position.
2. He should be a good aggressive rebounder.
3. He should have a good hook shot and some good baseline moves.
4. If he can hit well from the corners and along the baseline, it helps.
5. He should be able to feed cutting and driving teammates.

The movements of No. 1, the "trigger" man of the offense, would be as shown in Diagram 4-2. He can pass and go outside No. 3. He can pass and go inside No. 3 or break straight in for a return pass as on a "sucker" play. He can also pass and go away from the pass setting up a screen for No. 4, the high pivot-post man, or for No. 2, the shallow wing-man.

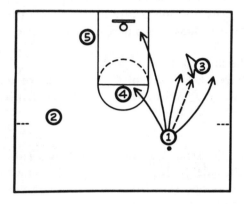

DIAGRAM 4-2

No. 1 and No. 3 may work an exchange of positions on shuttle moves (see Diagram 4-3). No. 4 and No. 5 constantly work on scissor moves to secure screens and picks for each other. The general rule is that if No. 4 moves to a low pivot-post position, then No. 5 always moves out to a high position. The pivot-post player in the low position may roam wide

DIAGRAM 4-3

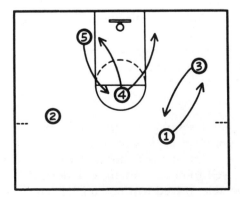

along the baseline, even to the corners if he desires. But he must move! The pivot-post player in the high position can play as high as the situation demands to adjust to the pressures of the defense, even beyond the top of the free throw circle. He may even play as wide as halfway to the sideline in his movements.

As shown in Diagram 4-4, if No. 1 dribbles over the top of No. 4 to secure a screen or a pick, No. 2 should hold his position until No. 1 is declared to a definite movement. No. 1 may use No. 4 for rub-off or screening options, but No. 2 must hold his action until the dribbler declares himself to a definite action or has passed the ball off. Once No. 1 has committed himself to the action shown, No. 2 may cut in the direction of the areas labeled "YES" by the arrows. He should never cut in the direction of the arrow labeled "NO." If he did, this would jam and crowd any possible openings or moves by No. 1 and No. 4.

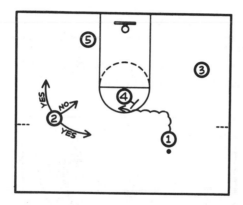

DIAGRAM 4-4

No. 1 should never try to pass the ball all the way from his starting position, which is split between No. 3 and No. 4, over to No. 2 (see Diagram 4-5). After dribbling to a position about even with No. 4, he should be in a safe passing area to make a pass to No. 2. Now with the ball in the No. 2 position, wingman No. 3 should go to the side of the ball. No. 4 and No. 5 can make the position moves shown and the offense is ready to be set up on the left side. No. 1 can drift to his right to the shallow wing position or he can move straight in toward the basket for a possible return pass and come back out to the shallow wing position if he is not open.

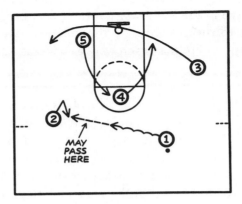

DIAGRAM 4-5

As illustrated in Diagram 4-6, No. 1 and No. 3 may work a shuttle along the sideline while No. 4 and No. 5 scissor for positions and openings. Here No. 1 passes to No. 3 and follows the pass outside. No. 3 dribbles the ball out to the No. 1 position and, *always turning to the inside on this move,* he is now in position to pass to No. 1 or to No. 5 or No. 4, if they should get open on their scissor moves.

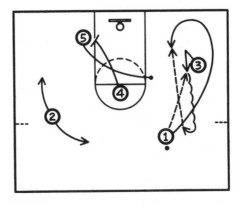

DIAGRAM 4-6

No. 1 may pass to No. 3 and follow for an inside screen and roll. In Diagram 4-7, No. 1 passes to No. 3 and follows the pass to the inside and screens for No. 3. No. 3 may drive to the inside off the screen or he may reverse and dribble toward the baseline and in for a drive or a roll-off option. Nos. 4, 5, and 2 watch for individual openings that may come from this move. They must wait until the movements of No. 1 and No. 3 are fully committed before making their cuts or they will jam the cutting lanes and any openings that may develop for No. 3 or No. 1.

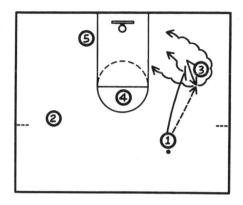

DIAGRAM 4-7

One of the fundamental cutting rules of this offense is that No. 1 may pass the ball to No. 3 and go away from his pass. In Diagram 4-8 he passes to No. 3 and moves away from the pass and in behind No. 4 to provide a screen for his cut to the baseline. If No. 4 is open, No. 3 will pass to him. As No. 4 goes to the low position, No. 5 comes out to the

DIAGRAM 4-8

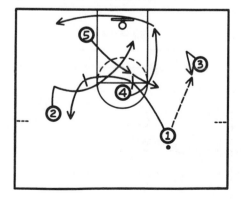

high position and No. 1 continues on to a position just to the left of the free throw lane where the can also furnish a set screen for No. 2 cutting in from the weak side for a possible opening.

Another fundamental principle of the offense is that when a player passes the ball into one of the pivot-post players, he should not always cut by that player, but rather he should vary his cuts and, at times, cut over or by the other pivot-post man. If the ball is passed to the low pivot-post, the player cuts over the high pivot-post. If the ball is passed to the high pivot-post, the cut may be by the low pivot-post. Also the pivot-past player without the ball is always alert to move into position to screen for a cutting player. In Diagram 4-9, No. 1 passes to No. 3 and holds. No. 3 passes into No. 5 on the low position; No. 4 moves out as shown, and No. 3 cuts over No. 4 for a screen and a possible opening.

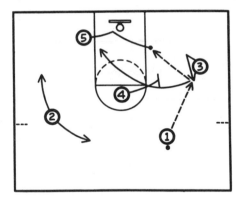

DIAGRAM 4-9

DIAGRAM 4-10

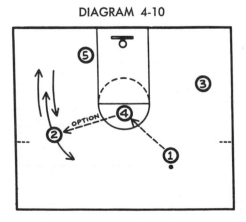

Any time the ball is passed into the high pivot-post position (in Diagram 4-10, it is No. 4), the first option he should look for is the pass to No. 2. No. 2 should always prowl the area and be ready for any sagging-off by the defense. When the defense sags-off, No. 2 can always take advantage of a good shot from this area.

When No. 1 drives through on a move or cuts out of his area, No. 2 comes out to take his place until No. 1 circulates back. As shown in Diagram 4-11, No. 1 passed to No. 3 and followed his pass to the outside. No. 4 and No. 5 on a scissor move frees No. 5 for a pass from No. 3. After passing to No. 5, No. 3 cuts over the top of No. 5 in following his pass. No. 2 comes out to the top of the circle to replace No. 1 driving through. If his defensive man is sagging, No. 5 should be alert to pass the ball to him for a possible shot from this area—one of the best percentage shooting areas on the floor.

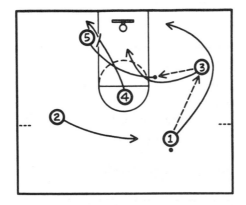

DIAGRAM 4-11

In Diagram 4-12, No. 1 passes to No. 3 and cuts straight in for a return pass. If open, No. 3 will pass to him. If not open No. 1 continues on through and provides a screen for No. 5 coming across the free throw lane. As No. 5 frees himself No. 3 passes him the ball and follows his pass. In the meantime, No. 2 has a sagging defensive player who has turned to watch the ball. No. 2 cuts through the back door for a possible sucker play and No. 5 may have the option of passing to No. 2 or No. 3 for openings. On this play, since No. 2 did not come out to replace No. 1 as a guard, No. 4 steps out to take over this responsibility until No. 1 has circulated back.

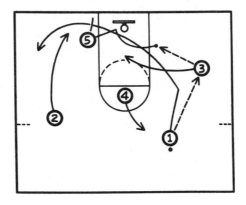

DIAGRAM 4-12

Definite rebounding responsibilities must be established. Nos. 3, 4, and 5 have the rebounding coverage responsibilities, as shown in Diagram 4-13, any time a shot goes up. The high pivot-post player covers the side opposite the low pivot-post man. The forward, or No. 3, covers the short middle area and No. 2 covers the long rebound and is always ready to

DIAGRAM 4-13

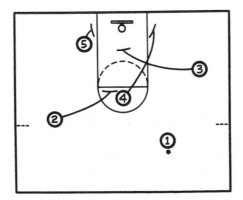

help No. 1 in defensing any fast break attempt. In some situations No. 4 and No. 3 may find it best to exchange rebounding responsibilities, with No. 4 going straight in and No. 3 covering his side.

Against a defense that is aggressive and spread out, the players in the 1-3-1 offense can just be spread out and spaced farther apart, giving them more freedom and free-lance opportunities. Nos. 1, 2, 3 and 4 can adjust their positions to spread the defense as they wish (see Diagram 4-14), and by faking and driving hard, they can use a "give and go" game for good openings from the same play situations as previously given. However, they search more for the one-on-one situations with no screen and roll or doubling options in this type of game against this kind of a defense.

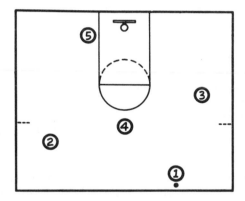

DIAGRAM 4-14

Against a defense that sags or sinks, the two pivot-post players simply play closer with the other players adjusting their positions accordingly (see Diagram 4-15). Against this type of defense No. 4 and No. 5 will engage in more scissor moves, and more screen and roll moves will be sought, with attempts being made to take advantage of the sagging defense at every opportunity.

GUIDING PRINCIPLES AND RULES FOR THE 1-3-1

When the 1-3-1 offense is operated as a free-lance offense, it becomes a rule game with certain guidelines to govern the movements of each player in specific situations. Here are some guiding principles for all players in general.

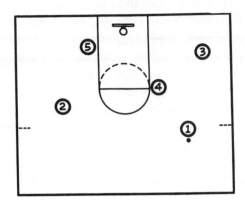

DIAGRAM 4-15

1. Keep the players spread as much as possible and especially the No. 1 and the No. 2 positions.
2. Keep the dribbler out of the middle. It is not a dribbling game and especially down the middle. This will jam the offense.
3. Pass the ball to either pivot-post player at every available opportunity.
4. It is an offense of movement. Keep all players moving to prevent sagging by the defense.
5. Rebounding responsibilities for players No. 3, 4, and 5 must be definitely established. No. 2 covers the long rebound responsibilities.
6. There are to be no second cutters by the pivot-post players. Do not jam the middle. Keep it open.
7. The pivot-post player that is free should move out to screen for cutting teammates.

Guiding principles for each individual player should be established so that they can exploit all free-lance opportunities. Here are the rules for each player and each position.

Player No. 1

If he passes to No. 3 he can do one of the following:

1. Follow the pass either inside or outside.
2. Play for the sucker drive straight in a quick return pass.
3. He may go away from the pass and screen for either No. 4 or No. 2 or both.
4. He may screen for the low pivot-post player.
5. He could cut over the high pivot-post and double back on a low pivot-post position himself.

If he passes the ball to Nos. 4 or 5, he has the options that he has when passing to No. 3. He could dribble off the high pivot-post for openings or for pass-off opportunities to No. 2.

Player No. 2

1. No. 2 should keep on the move and prowl his area.
2. He must be alert to replace No. 1 when he drives and goes inside on the offense.
3. As a weak side player he must be alert for opportunities to break over or by the free pivot-post player for scoring opportunities.
4. He should be constantly alert for backside baseline cuts and moves.
5. He can even go in and pivot-post when the opportunity presents itself.
6. He must not stand still.
7. He must be alert for shooting opportunities that can come to him as a result of a sagging defense. He is expected to hit well from his area.

Player No. 3

1. Be alert for driving opportunities.
2. Feed the pivot-post players at every opportunity.
3. Cut by the pivot-post players at every opportunity.
4. After feeding the ball to a teammate, go somewhere—MOVE!
5. Shuttle moves and two-on-two opportunities can be worked with No. 1.
6. Shoot when open in his operational area.
7. Feed all cutters and be especially alert for weak side moves by players away from the ball.
8. This player must rebound hard on all shots.

Player No. 4

1. This player roams the outer half of the free throw circle and outside to an area as wide as halfway to the sideline.
2. He should work constant scissor and screening movements with No. 5. They constantly exchange positions.
3. He replaces No. 1 when both No. 1 and No. 2 go inside on moves.
4. He should be alert to move out and screen for teammates cutting when No. 5 or No. 3 has the ball.
5. He should drive and shoot at every opportunity.
6. When pivot-posting with the ball he feeds cutting teammates.
7. When he receives the ball on the high pivot-post position, his first look is to see if No. 2 is open, then to check for other opportunities.
8. He must rebound hard on all shots.

Player No. 5

1. He prowls his operational area along the baseline for openings.
2. He constantly exchanges positions with his pivot-post teammate No. 4 and works scissor and screening moves with him.
3. When pivot-posting with the ball he feeds cutting teammates.
4. When his teammate No. 4 has the ball in the pivot-post position, he moves out to screen for cutting teammates.
5. He must drive and shoot at every opportunity.
6. He must more than assume his responsibilties for offensive rebounding.

BASIC OFFENSIVE PATTERNS

The 1-3-1 offense given up to this point has been one of freedom and movement with guiding principles and rules providing free-lance opportunities according to the abilities of the players in the various positions. This offense in itself is an excellent one, but if the coach feels the need for more disciplined or a more formalized attack, it can be made to be so. The following basic offensive play patterns lend themselves to the more disciplined and structured offense while blending well with the free-lance game that can be played from the 1-3-1 attack.

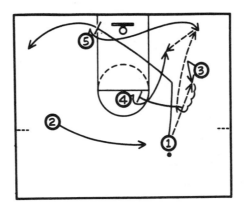

DIAGRAM 4-16

Diagram 4-16 should be a quick opener play. No. 1 passes to No. 3 and breaks in toward the basket. If he is not open he continues across the free-throw lane and screens for No. 5. If No. 5 is open, No. 3 passes to him in close, but if not open, No. 3 dribbles out for adjustment and then turns and passes in to No. 5 who has now moved out toward the corner along the baseline. No. 5 may take opportunities to drive or shoot from this position also. After passing to No. 5, No. 3 moves in behind No. 4 for a screen and No. 4 cuts sharply behind No. 3 down the side of the free throw lane. This could give a quick opener for No. 4 and if he is open, No. 5 feeds him the ball. If No. 4 is not open, No. 5 passes the ball outside to No. 2 and the players can quickly re-form by filling the positions and carrying the play or the offense to the left side of the floor.

In Diagram 4-17, No. 1 passes to No. 3 and after cutting straight in for the basket, turns right in behind No. 3. No. 3 turns and passes to No. 1 along the baseline and then moves in behind No. 4 for a screen. No. 4 cuts down the free throw lane for a quick opener. If he is not open he goes on through and No. 3 continues on down the lane to screen for No. 5 on the low pivot-post. No. 5 cuts sharply off the screen and if he is open, No. 1 feeds him and follows his pass for another possible quick opener. If no scoring opportunity results from this, the ball is passed outside and the offense is set up again.

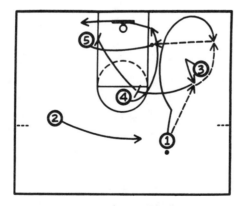

DIAGRAM 4-17

A double screen can very easily be set up for the weak side player and, as shown in Diagram 4-18, No. 1 passes to No. 3 and moves away from the pass setting a screen behind the high pivot-post man, No. 4. No. 4 cuts down the lane and not being open, pulls up along the baseline toward the corner and comes out enough to receive the ball from No. 3. No. 5 and No. 1 now move in a position along the left side of the free-throw lane in a tight position together so that No. 2 cutting by them will have a double screen formed for him. He may cut over or behind them for an opening.

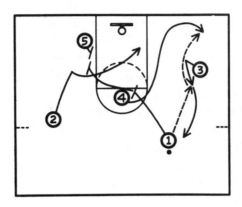

DIAGRAM 4-18

Double screens and picks can be worked into the offense very well. In Diagram 4-19, No. 1 passes to No. 3, follows to the outside, and pulls up short and stops to the side and in front of No. 3. No. 3 passes the ball back to him and rolls out toward the basket for a possible opening and screens for No. 5, the low pivot-post man coming across the free-throw lane. Not being open immediately, No. 5 moves out along the baseline toward the corner where No. 1 passes him the ball. Now No. 1 moves in

DIAGRAM 4-19

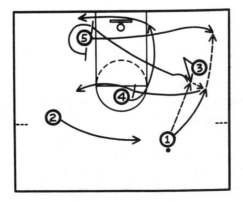

behind No. 4 for a screen and a possible quick opening. If not open, he continues on across the free-throw lane to team up with No. 3 for the double pick. Diagram 4-20, Phase 2, will give this opening.

The players have now arrived at the positions shown in Diagram 4-20 and No. 5 has the ball. No. 5 quickly passes the ball outside to No. 2 who quickly moves it over to No. 1. After passing off, No. 5 moves quickly along the baseline and across the free-throw lane and in behind No. 4 and No. 3 who have moved in tight shoulder to shoulder to form a double screen for No. 5. No. 1 passes No. 5 the ball for a jump shot or a drive around Nos. 4 and 3. If No. 5 is not open he moves across the free-throw lane and No. 4 quickly moves out from behind No. 3 for a quick opening or a drive.

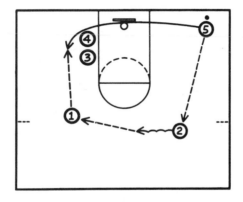

DIAGRAM 4-20

Taking advantage of the possibilities that can result from the scissor movements between the pivot-post players No. 4 and No. 5 is much to the advantage of the offense. In Diagram 4-21 some of the possibilities are shown. No. 1 passes to No. 3 and moves in. No. 4 moves out for a possible high pivot-post reception, but not being open, moves immediately into a scissor move on the opposite side of the free-throw lane with No. 5. No. 5 could cut sharply off this scissor move for openings. He may also delay and move across the lane cutting off No. 1's move across the lane for a possible opening in closer to the basket. No. 3 could pass to him here if he is open. If no openings come from this, No. 3 can pass the ball outside to No. 2 and now No. 1 could scissor off possible screening moves around

No. 4 and be open. Also, No. 4 could move down the lane or across the lane in a scissor move again to secure a screen for No. 5 as he breaks out toward the ball as it changes sides. With practice, the timing on these moves can be perfected and will work for fine scoring opportunities.

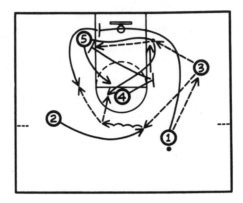

DIAGRAM 4-21

To meet any and all defenses, the 1-3-1 offense is probably one of the best all-purpose offenses yet devised.

5

The Illinois
Continuity Offense

There have been many great minds in basketball. Some have received more publicity and credit than others. A coach speaking at a clinic once said, "There are only two classes of basketball coaches. They are either imitators or innovators." One such mind belonging to the class of innovator is that of Coach Vernon Drenckpohl. He is the innovator of the offense presented in this chapter. Vernon coached high school basketball at Clayton, Argenta, Vandalia, and Sycamore, Illinois over a period of 28 years. During this time he was highly successful as a coach, but more importantly he had a profound influence on basketball and the young men he coached, many of whom entered the coaching profession. Being a native of Centralia, Illinois, he was a pupil of the famous "King" Arthur Trout who coached Centralia teams for 37 years. During that time Trout coached three Centralia teams to Illinois State High School championships. Being an apt basketball pupil, Drenckpohl found himself on one of the basketball squads at the University of Illinois during the days of Craig Ruby. Always the loyal "Illini" and always the pupil of Coach Trout, his style and innovations in basketball have been copied and imitated by many coaches throughout the state and the mid-west. In associating an offense with Coach Vernon Drenckpohl, only two words could come to the mind—"Illinois" and "Continuity," thus the name Illinois Continuity Offense.

The fundamental thought and philosophy underlying this offense is that, no matter where the ball goes or where it is passed, the player with the ball will have the opportunity for continuous multiple options with the four remaining teammates which will result from the moves that all five players make. This is the basic objective of the offense, and the purpose is to keep a continuous flow and movement of both the players and the ball, the result of which will bring possible scoring opportunities with almost every maneuver.

The offense requires good movement of all players in all positions. The offense does not require a pivot-post player of extreme size. However, if the pivot-post player is big and can move well, it is an added advantage, of course, but the offense is not necessarily dependent upon the pivot-post position as being all important. Good execution of the movements by the player in this position is as necessary as movement in the other positions; consequently it makes relatively little difference whether this player is large or small, providing he can perform his task well and make the necessary moves demanded by the offense.

To begin the offense, the players line up as shown in Diagram 5-1. No. 5 may vary his starting position from the outer half of the free throw circle to any place along the free throw lane. There is an advantage on many of the options to station him just above the free throw line. This is true because when he is moving back at an angle, he is more likely to be able to pivot and move toward the basket after receiving the ball, since he is moving his defensive man more and the angle of movement from this position does not allow the defensive player to get as good a position on the moving pivot-post player.

Players No. 3 and 4 are the forwards, and are shown to be stationed about even with the free throw line extended. They start their operations farther back, and from these positions employ fakes to get loose and to receive passes from the guards. They must be moving up to meet the passes made by the guards, and should not be any farther up than the area shown in the diagram when they expect to receive the ball.

Players No. 1 and 2 are the guards. They position themselves for their base of operations as shown in Diagram 5-1. The offense may operate to either the right or the left side of the floor equally well. The diagrams give the operational move to one side only. The reader must always keep in mind that the same play can be used on the opposite side of the floor.

If the guard, No. 1 should pass the ball to No. 3, he has these options: 1) He may go inside No. 3; 2) He may go outside No. 3.

The pivot-post player, No. 5, watches the guard, No. 1. The move that No. 5 makes will be determined by the option that No. 1 takes, specifically whether he goes to the outside or inside of No. 3. If No. 1 passes to No. 3 and breaks to the inside of No. 3, then No. 5 will go behind the ball to Position A shown in Diagram 5-1. If No. 1 passes to

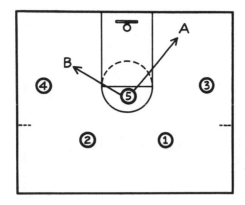

DIAGRAM 5-1

No. 3 and drives to the outside of No. 3, or if he dribbles to the outside of No. 3, then No. 5 goes to Position B away from the ball. These are the two basic guard options in the offense, and they determine the movement of No. 5 as to whether he moves to Position A or B.

The First Guard Option

The forward can determine the option the guard takes by his own position on the floor. If the forward wants the guard to go inside, he should position himself closer to the sideline when he received the ball so as to give the guard plenty of room to maneuver between the forward and the free throw lane. If No. 3 is to receive the pass, he should fake his defensive man out of position and be coming to meet the ball somewhat closer to the sideline so as not to narrow the width of the lane through which No. 1 will be breaking, as shown in Diagram 5-2. As soon as No. 5 knows the guard is taking the inside option, he moves to Position A as shown. He is the first cutter on the play. Guard No. 1, cutting inside, will be more likely to receive a return pass from No. 3, if after passing to No. 3, No. 1 will break more toward the free throw lane, and not too close to No. 3. He should also move at full speed. If No. 1 should receive the return pass from No. 3, he either dribbles in for a shot, or he may pass off to either No. 4 or 5. If No. 1 goes in for a shot, No. 4 and 5 both come in for rebounds and No. 3 follows his pass. No. 2 now comes over to the middle of the floor to be ready for a possible pass out from No. 3, and also to be back for defense should the ball be intercepted.

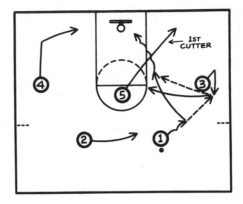

DIAGRAM 5-2

After receiving the initial pass from No. 1, No. 3 needs only a quick glance to determine if No. 1 is open for a return pass. If he is not, then No. 3 looks for his second option which is a pass to No. 5 breaking down toward Position A (Diagram 5-1). The pivot-post player, No. 5 has been watching No. 1, and as soon as he sees that No. 1 is going to make the break inside of No. 3, No. 5 breaks for Position A, getting toward this spot ahead of the break by No. 1, so that No. 1 has a clear area in which to drive for the basket. On this move, No. 5 may vary the distance he breaks behind the ball. He may break just along the lane, or widen out. If the team is not blessed with a tall center, it could be desirable to move out wider. If No. 5 should be guarded by the opponent's tall man, and he goes out wider taking the defensive man with him away from the basket, it could be an advantage especially when the team has good rebounding forwards.

If No. 1 is not open for a return pass, No. 3 then looks over his shoulder towards No. 5 for the second option. The idea here is to pass to No. 5 somewhere in the area shown in Diagram 5-3, as he is making the angle cut to Position A. If the ball can be passed to him at this point, it will be difficult for the defense to position on him, and many times he can pivot toward the end line and drive for the basket. He can also fake this pivot toward the end line, reverse back in the opposite direction, and drive for the basket. He could also shoot from Position A, if he found himself open as he pulled out a little wider on this move. No. 3 after passing to No. 5 breaks toward the basket. If No. 5 shoots, Nos. 1, 4 and 3 are in good rebound position, and a shot from this area is a fine percentage shot. No. 4 must be cautioned to remain on his side of the floor until the options with Nos. 1, 5, and 3 have been exhausted. If he should break into the area too soon he will clog the area and thereby prevent any further options from being undertaken.

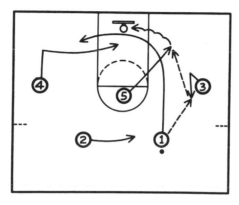

DIAGRAM 5-3

If, at the time No. 5 moves toward Position A and at a time the ball is passed to No. 3, the defensive player moves over in front of him to keep him from receiving the pass from No. 3, No. 5 should break a little wider, stop quickly, reverse toward the basket for a pass from No. 3, as shown in Diagram 5-4.

DIAGRAM 5-4

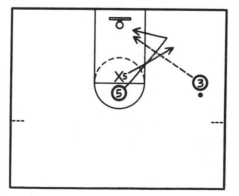

If No. 5 does not have an opportunity for a shot, and if he does not use a reverse pivot and then drive to the basket, he will no doubt be drawn somewhat farther out to the side of the floor near the base line. He now looks for his second option, which is a return pass to No. 3, who drives in for a shot, as shown in Diagram 5-5. On this cut, No. 3 should be cautioned not to break too close to No. 5, but rather to stay far enough away so as to provide ample space for the drive to the basket. If No. 5 sees that No. 3 is not open for a return pass on his break for the basket, No. 5 should start looking for his third option, which is a pass to No. 4.

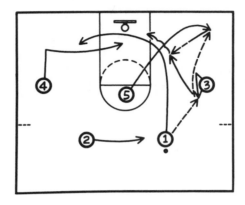

DIAGRAM 5-5

No. 4 seeing the play started by No. 1, with No. 1 moving to the opposite side of the floor, now makes an adjustment or movement toward the end line, allowing No. 3 to make his pass to No. 5 and his break for the basket. No. 4 now makes his break across the free throw lane with the expectation of receiving a pass from No. 5, which will result in a possible shot. This maneuver is shown in Diagram 5-6. If No. 4 does not have a shot, he may make a return pass to No. 5, who after passing to No. 4, immediately cuts behind No. 4 for a return pass. No. 5 may continue the drive toward the basket for a shot, or stop behind a screen set by No. 4 and as a result be in position for a good jump shot. If No. 5 sees that No. 4 is not open for a pass on this third option, he passes the ball to No. 2 at the guard position and then breaks toward his original position on the free throw line. As a result of this movement, and with the adjustments which are made by No. 1 and 3, the team will maintain the necessary floor balance with a forward stationed on each side of the floor and the pivot-post player once more stationed in the middle and at the outer half of the free throw circle. Diagram 5-7 shows how these maneuvers will bring about proper floor balance and bring the players into the proper position to begin the offense over again, or enable the players to begin another phase of the continuity pattern dependant upon the defensive tactics of the opponents. If No. 5 thinks it is difficult to get the pass out to No. 2 from his position at A along the base line, he should look again for No. 4 who should continue his path as shown in Diagram 5-7. If No. 4 continues this path far enough to the sideline, he is sure to be open for a pass from No. 5. No. 4 can then relay the ball out to No. 2.

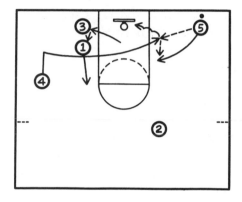

DIAGRAM 5-6

DIAGRAM 5-7

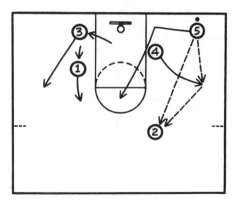

Diagram 5-8 shows that No. 2 should not come over any farther in the right half of the court than is necessary for him to receive the pass out from either No. 4 or No. 5. It would be ideal if he could remain in the middle of the court to receive this pass. If he has to come too far over to the right, it will be difficult for him to get a pass over to the left side of the floor. Also if No. 2 dribbles over to the left, the defense will have time to shift over with him. Therefore as soon as the pass from either No. 4 or No. 5 is received by No. 2, he should pass the ball immediately to No. 1, who has completed his hook on his original move as shown in Diagram 5-7, and now is in the position shown in Diagram 5-8. This position is just outside the free throw lane, and about even with the free throw line. It is important that No. 1, after his first pass to No. 3 as shown in Diagrams 5-2 and 5-3, drive all the way to the basket and then hook back to the described area. This will give No. 1 many good jump shots from this position, since the defensive player will not guard him as closely as a result of his hook move away from the basket. If No. 1 merely wants to make this move in the easy way, and go almost in a straight line from his original position to this spot, he will not be open very often for a pass and a shot. After No. 5 passes to either No. 2 or No. 4, he should break to the positions shown in Diagram 5-8. No. 2 takes a quick look for No. 1 as No. 1 executes the hook maneuver, and if No. 1 is not open, No. 2 then looks for the pivot-post man, No. 5, and may pass to him enabling him to obtain a good shot. After No. 4 passes to No. 2, he breaks toward and past the basket expecting a possible pass from No. 1 (see Diagram 5-8). This pass could also come from No. 5, if No. 2 chooses to pass to the pivot-

DIAGRAM 5-8

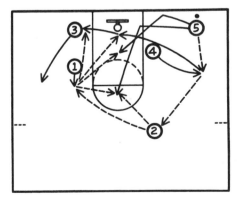

post man as he cuts in, instead of to No. 1. It is a basic rule or principle of this offense that if a forward or a guard should pass the ball back to the guard position as shown, that forward or guard making the pass out to the guard position, and in this case to No. 2, follows the path as shown for No. 4 in Diagram 5-8.

After No. 5 passes the ball out from his deep position (Position A, see Diagrams 5-7 and 5-8) to No. 2 or by relaying the ball to No. 4 and then to No. 2, he breaks toward his original position on the free throw line. This will station the players in the positions shown in Diagram 5-9. This maneuver has cleared the right side of the floor for a drive by No. 2. When No. 2 drives for the basket, No. 1 should come out in the front of the free throw circle to give defensive floor balance. No. 4 and 5 are now in good rebound positions. No. 5 may also do a pick and roll as No. 2 dribbles past him.

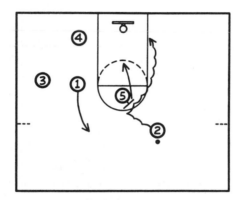

DIAGRAM 5-9

Another option resulting from this situation will enable No. 2 while out in front in the guard position to pass to No. 1, and then break to the right side of the floor toward the basket. As a result of this maneuver, No. 1 could pass to No. 5, who in turn could pass to No. 2 on a "Sucker" play, or a back door maneuver as shown in Diagram 5-10.

CLEARING OPTIONS

The two options shown in Diagrams 5-9 and 5-10 are "Clearing Options" and are made possible by applying the principle or rule that, every

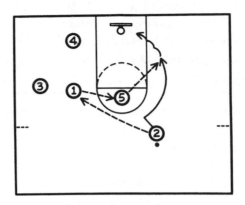

DIAGRAM 5-10

time the ball is passed back to the guard position, the forward (which in this instance is No. 4) will make the cut as shown in Diagram 5-8, thereby clearing the area and enabling the guard No. 2 to make his drive to the basket. However if it is decided not to clear one side of the floor, the "Clearing Option" could be "bypassed" by having No. 4 ignore the "rule cut" and, when the ball is passed out to No. 2 from either No. 5 or No. 4, No. 4 could stay on this side of the floor. As a result, the offense would then have a forward on each side of the floor, the pivot-post player No. 5 breaking to the free throw line once more, one guard, No. 2 out in front, and the other guard, No. 1, completing the hook. If No. 1 does not receive a pass from No. 2, he will come back out in front. This will place the players in the starting positions once more, except that the guards and forwards will be on opposite sides of the floor from their original starting positions. In this offense the guards and forwards will work from both sides of the floor and the guards can often start the offense out in front by a cross or an exchange maneuever before making the original pass into the forwards. If No. 1, after receiving a pass on the completion of the hook, does not have an option or an opening pass to any other player, he can pass back out to No. 2, or he may dribble back out to a position in front of the circle.

The Third Forward Option

Everything that happened in the offense as shown in Diagrams 5-3 through 5-10 was the result of No. 3, the forward, passing to No. 5, and the options that came as a result of that pass. The third option is begun by a pass to No. 4 from No. 3 as shown in Diagram 5-11. After receiving the original pass from the guard No. 1, No. 3 takes a quick glance at this

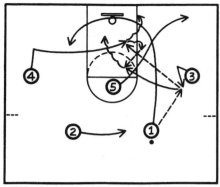

DIAGRAM 5-11

first option, which is a pass to No. 1 who is cutting toward the basket, and then his second option, which is a pass to No. 5. If neither of these players are free to receive the pass, then No. 3 looks for the third forward option, a pass to No. 4. No. 4 must delay his break until the last moment, and then break hard into the center of the floor as shown in Diagram 5-11. No. 3 passes to No. 4, who may go in for a shot or execute a jump shot at any time he is able to do so. After passing to No. 4, No. 3 breaks across behind No. 4 for a return pass. If he receives the pass he may drive in for a layup, or stop and take a jump shot. Also, when No. 3 receives this return pass, No. 4 may roll and drive for the basket looking for a return pass from No. 3.

The Fourth Forward Option

The fourth forward option is shown in Diagram 5-12. No. 3 after receiving the initial pass from No. 1, passes back to the other guard, No. 2 who has moved over to receive the pass. No. 2 can pass to No. 1 coming out on the hook, or to the pivot-post man, No. 5 as shown in the diagram.

DIAGRAM 5-12

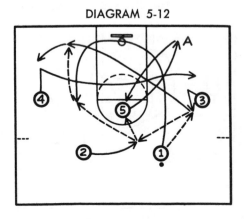

No. 1 may take a jump shot, or pass to No. 3, who after passing to the guard, No. 2, follows the basic "rule cut" of breaking toward and past the basket as shown again in Diagram 5-12. No. 1 may also pass to No. 5 breaking out from Position A to the free throw line. If this pass should be made to No. 5, or if No. 5 should receive a pass from No. 2, the "Clearing Options" shown in Diagrams 5-9 and 5-10 are again possible. If No. 1, after completing the hook, and receiving the pass from No. 2, is not open, and cannot pass to either No. 3 or 5, he continues his path on out in front or to the guard position with a dribble. No. 3 will continue his path up the side to the original forward position, and with No. 4 moving across the floor as shown in Diagram 5-12, all five players are ready to start the series again as the floor balance has been accomplished. This can be done because there is continuous movement of the players without any hesitation or rearrangement of personnel. This in turn results in a successful continuity pattern of play.

To develop the offense, and to get timing and smoothness into the continuity pattern, it would be practical to have the players practice passing the ball into the forward and back out to the guard at least three times before running the series through for a shot at the basket. This would give the team practice in running the pattern and help them know the options that are possible. In a game situation, this would not be practical of course.

In this series and in the fourth forward option, the defensive player guarding No. 2 may try to play him close and pressure him to prevent No. 3 from passing the ball out to him. If this occurs, it will open up the area in back of No. 2's defensive man, and make it easier for No. 3 to pass to No. 4 as No. 4 breaks across the floor. Also if this option to No. 4 does not materialize, No. 1, after completing the hook maneuver, can break toward No. 3. No. 3 can now pass to No. 1 instead of passing out to No. 2, as shown in Diagram 5-13. No. 1 may take whatever opening that results

DIAGRAM 5-13

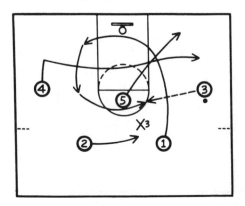

from the pass, or he may take the ball outside for balancing purposes
of starting the offense and the series over again.

The Second Guard Option

The second option that the guard No. 1 may take after passing to
No. 3 is to go outside the forward No. 3, as shown in Diagram 5-14. (No. 2

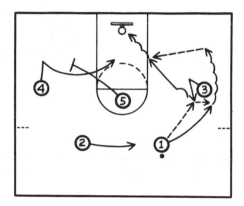

DIAGRAM 5-14

would have this option if the play went to the left side.) The forward, No.
3 may determine this play, or set it up by moving in closer to the free
throw lane, thus giving No. 1 more room to cut and maneuver to the
outside. The position of No. 3 on the floor could actually be the determining factor as to whether the first or second guard option will be used.
No. 1 may also pass to No. 3 and then receive a return pass after cutting to
the outside of No. 3. No. 3 may execute a pick and roll and drive to the
basket with the expectation of receiving a return pass from No. 1. These
maneuvers will require a quick defensive shift by the players guarding
No. 1 and 3 and will place No. 3 in a good rebounding position. No. 5,
the pivot-post player, seeing No. 1 cut to the outside of the forward, No. 3,
now breaks to the opposite side of the floor and away from the ball to
Position B as shown in Diagram 5-1. This maneuver by No. 5 sets up a
pick for No. 4. Another possible option is shown in Diagram 5-15. Instead
of passing the ball back to No. 1 as he cuts to the outside, No. 3 could
fake to him as he goes by, then move quickly to the inside using one or
two quick dribbles and execute a quick bounce pass to No. 1 as shown
in Diagram 5-15. No. 1 would then be in good position to continue on
to the basket for the layup shot.

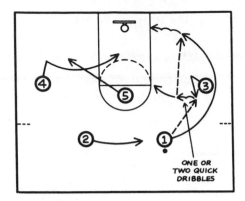

DIAGRAM 5-15

If on the initial move, No. 1 receives the ball from No. 3 as he cuts past him and is unable to make the pass to No. 3 on the pick and roll maneuver, he then continues to drive toward the end line instead, and looks first for No. 4 coming off No. 5's pick as shown in Diagram 5-16. No. 5 in this situation, seeing No. 4 going in for a shot, should reverse back to the middle to be in rebound position. No. 3 is already in good rebound position. If No. 1 cannot pass to No. 4, he then should look for a possible pass to No. 5 who is now breaking toward the ball after the break by No. 4. If No. 4 is not open for a pass from No. 1, he should move out to the forward position as shown in Diagram 5-16, where he will be able to take a pass from No. 1 should it be necessary to do so in order to get the ball out of the corner and away from the baseline. If No. 1 passes to either No. 4 or 5, he immediately cuts behind them for a

DIAGRAM 5-16

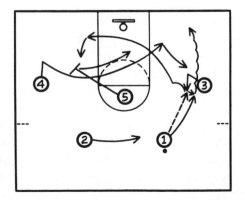

possible return pass. If he receives the pass he may drive for the basket or execute a jump shot over the screen set by either No. 4 or 5 as shown in Diagram 5-17.

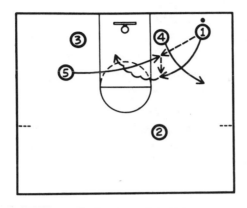

DIAGRAM 5-17

DIAGRAM 5-18

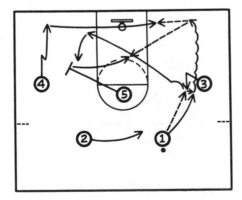

The Back Door Option

Another option which is possible as a result of the maneuvers shown in Diagrams 5-14 through 5-17 is known as the "Back Door" option. This option is shown in Diagram 5-18, and has proven to be a good one since it provides good scoring opportunities. It should be used often. When No. 4 sees No. 1 cutting to the outside of No. 3, he, instead of breaking off the pick set by No. 5, continues to slide down toward the end line. At the proper time, No. 4 then breaks across the floor just in front of the basket, expecting a pass from No. 1. In this case, when No. 5 sees that No. 4 has dropped into a deep position along the baseline, he breaks away from the ball, and then straight back toward the ball again. This break should be timed so that No. 4 and No. 5 are coming across the free throw lane (as shown in Diagram 5-18) at practically the same time, which will give No. 1 an opportunity to pass to either player.

If No. 1 cannot use any of the options shown in Diagrams 5-14 through 5-18, he should then pass the ball out to No. 2 at the guard position. (He could relay it out to No. 2 via No. 4 if necessary.) No. 2 has a possible opportunity to pass to No. 3 who has completed the hook after his cut toward the basket and come back out along the free throw lane. This is the same hook pattern that No. 1 takes on the first guard option when the guard goes inside on his cut after passing to the forward. No. 2 could also pass to No. 5 as shown in Diagram 5-19. If No. 2's pass is made to No. 3, No. 3 may have a good shot. If No. 3 does not shoot he may pass to No. 1 who after passing the ball out to No. 2, moves to Position A as shown in Diagram 5-19. No. 3 may also pass to No. 5, who had previously cut toward No. 1 and not receiving the ball, will be positioned to the right of the free throw lane where he stays until No. 3 receives the pass from No. 2 as he completes the hook from the basket area. It must be

DIAGRAM 5-19

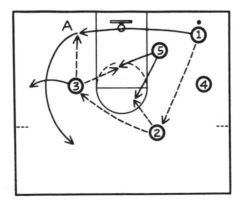

remembered here that, when No. 3 executes the pick, roll, and hook movement enabling him to receive the ball at the end of the hook, he has accessibility to all the same options that No. 1 had on the first guard option when he broke inside of No. 3, and as shown in Diagrams 5-8, 5-9, 5-10, 5-12, and 5-13.

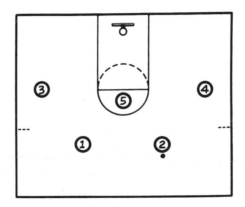

DIAGRAM 5-20

If none of these option possibilities develop, No. 3 can pass the ball back out to No. 2, and then slide out to the regular forward position on the same side of the floor in which he is now stationed. If No. 1 does not receive a pass from No. 3, he continues on out to a guard position. The players are now in the regular starting position as shown in Diagram 5-20, except that the guards and forwards have exchanged positions and are now on opposite sides of the floor. Going back to Diagram 5-19, if No. 2 is unable to pass to No. 3 or 5, he should attempt to pass to No. 4, and start either the first or second guard option plays again as has been previously described. He may also pass the ball to No. 1 who could start the option series to the left side of the floor also, remembering that this continuity series can be executed on either the right or left side of the floor equally well.

ADVANTAGES OF THE OFFENSE

One of the best or outstanding features of the Illinois Continuity offense is the good offensive rebounding position of the players after a shot is taken. In nearly all instances there will be a triangle of offensive players near the basket for offensive rebounds. Teams that use this offense have had very good offensive rebound records.

The continuity flow of the pattern is excellent and provides for continuous movement of both the ball and the players. It exerts constant pressure on the defense, and results in many scoring opportunities at frequent intervals.

The offensive pattern while providing good rebounding coverage at all times, also has good defensive balance should the ball be lost to the opposition at any given time during the maneuevers.

The offense can, with little change of movement and floor coverage be very effective against a zone defense. Looking closely at the options shown in Diagram 5-12, it can be seen that both good movement and overload possibilities are present for use against the zone defenses.

This offense lends itself well to the use of breakdown drills for teaching the various options as the entire squad can be used in these drills. This is an advantage over just running the starting five through the options while neglecting the reserves with a workout that is not enough for them to develop the needed experience they should have in learning the offense. Using these drills for pre-season workouts will give the squad practice in ball handling and shooting while teaching the entire squad the offensive pattern and its continuity movement with all its options.

6

The Rotation Offense

The Rotation offense was conveived and developed in 1949 by Dr. William Healey while coaching at Eastern Illinois University at Charleston, Illinois. (A book entitled *Basketball's Rotation Offense* published by Interstate Publishing and Printing Company of Danville, Illinois, was placed on the market in 1964 and gives a detailed breakdown of the many options comprising this offense.) With this offense Dr. Healey's teams established fabulous records, winning 388 of 576 games during a twenty-eight year coaching career. These wins brought about six college conference championships, five state college championships, two National Association of Intercollegiate Athletics Holiday Tournament Championships, as well as other honors.

The Rotation offense is a pattern offense and a disciplined offense. It is successful because it has continuity, one unsuccessful maneuver followed by another maneuver which will be successful without any stopping of action or changing of floor positions by the players. In any pattern offense, continuous movement of players in a predetermined plan is essential if the offense is to be successful. The Rotation offense is a team offense and its success depends upon the cooperation of all players so that the high percentage shot is obtained. While it may appear that only two players are collaborating to obtain the good shot, other players are executing moves and screens which will result in a teammate eventually being freed for the high percentage shot if one of the first two players is not successful.

The Rotation offense is primarily a screening offense with every player screening when he does not have the ball. All players should be "screen conscious" as the success of the offense is based primarily on screening. This should be uppermost in the minds of all players and they should be made to believe that, with screens executed by practically every player, eventually the high percentage shot will be obtained. The players are moving constantly and are screening at every opportunity. By working for the high percentage shot it is possible for the average shooter to be consistently successful. The player should develop judgment as to whether or not he has the high percentage shot and this will come about by constant practice and a belief in the offense.

THE THEORY BEHIND THE ROTATION

The basic purpose or theory regarding the Rotation offense is to force or push the defense back under the basket so that the 15 to 18 foot jump shot from behind the screen may be obtained. Constant movement and screening by the players will jam the defense and enable the offensive players to gain good shooting position. The players must adhere to this theory at all times. Failure to do so will result in a breakdown in the pattern of play because of lack of continuity. When this happens the basic principles which determine the success of the pattern are destroyed and the offense cannot function properly. Every player has a job to do and must do it. The success of the offense depends to a great extent on the player without the ball. Proper timing determines the success of the offense and the inability of one player to do his part completely destroys the continuity and effectiveness of the Rotation. Each player must perform his task at the proper time to assure the continuity of play.

ADVANTAGES OF THE ROTATION

The advantages of the Rotation offense may be listed as follows:

1. Better rebounding because the rebounders are in good position.
2. The players know approximately when the shot will be taken and can maneuver for rebounding position quickly.
3. The coach has control of his players as they must fit into their position; otherwise, the continuity will be destroyed. The players know this.
4. The offense makes for teamwork.
5. The offense can be broken down into separate parts for easy teaching.
6. The separate parts can be used as specific drills, which, when put together, is the offense.
7. The offense makes the average shooter a threat because he can get the good shot.
8. Players have definite assignments.
9. The offense provides an opportunity for all five players to score.

10. The offense provides for individual abilities.
11. The offense requires constant player movement.
12. The offense makes it impossible to double team any one player.

PLAYER POSITION AND MOVEMENT

The most important element in any offense is the positioning and movement of the players. In the Rotation offense the players are constantly moving, virtually without pause or delay, until the desired high percentage shot is obtained. The offense is so designed that, should a player not be able to obtain the desired shot, there is no need for regrouping because each player moves into his next position and the continuity of play is sustained until another opportunity for a shot presents itself.

Every player is important to the success of the offense even though he does not have the ball. The player should be made to realize that every movement he makes, whether he has the ball or not, has a definite purpose and will have a direct bearing on the success of the pattern. The offense does provide for a certain amount of free play (which must be a part of every pattern offense) and players are encouraged to use their individual abilities in this freedom of action. This initiative on the part of the players is permissable and should be encouraged. The pattern should not be followed so closely that it destroys the individual abilities of the players to act on their own should the opportunity present itself. This phase of the game is impossible to defend against. If the player's effort to use his own initiative does not materialize, he should quickly adjust his movements to coincide with those required in the continuity pattern.

Continuity of Play

The success of any pattern play depends on continuity which means that it should be possible to continue the pattern of play until the desired shot is obtained. The Rotation offense requires perfect floor balance at all times and, if this is strictly adhered to, continuity of play will not be a problem. Every player should attempt with every movement to set up a teammate for the high percentage shot by the use of a proper screen or a good pass. This type of cooperation by all the players makes it possible to have balanced team scoring and fosters good team morale because each player knows that his success depends to a very large extent upon the efforts of his teammates. He also knows that he must work hard in an effort to help his teammate to score if he expects help in return.

Each player, with the exception of the center, is able to play every position. Consequently, each must know what his teammates are doing at all times thereby enabling him to time his movements to coincide with his teammates. Learning all the positions poses a problem early in the teaching of this offense as the player must be able to understand the purpose of the offense from the very beginning. He must become acquainted with the basic requirements of all the positions. He will learn the other requirements very quickly. Naturally every player wants to score. However, he should realize of what importance the player without the ball is to the total offense as well as the player with the ball in efforts to obtain the high percentage shot. The player must also realize that continuity of play is necessary if he, in turn, is to obtain the ball and the opportunity to shoot.

ESTABLISHING PROPER FLOOR BALANCE

The most important single element in the Rotation offense is establishing and maintaining proper floor balance. As all the players, with the exception of the center, are required to play all the positions, it may be difficult at first to learn all the movements necessary for all positions. However the movements required for all these positions are basically the same and the players can quickly learn these movements. By so doing, players can maintain the proper floor balance once they grasp the basic idea of the rotation pattern. The basic idea, of course, is to push the defense back under the basket so the 15 to 18 foot jump shot from behind the screen may be obtained.

Importance of Shooting

No player can score unless he can shoot. Shooting in basketball is very important. However it is also true that the better the shot, the better chance there is of making it. Every shot should be taken under the best conditions possible to assure its being successful. If the shot is taken under the same conditions each time, a higher percentage of the shots obtained will be successful.

The theory behind the Rotation offense in regard to shooting is to push the defense back under the basket in a compact fashion so that the shooter can get the 15 to 18 foot jump shot from behind the screen. If the shot is always taken from approximately the same distance from the basket, the shooter will be more accurate. The free throw is a good example of this theory. The longer the Rotation is run, and the more movement taking place by the players, the better the chances of setting up the high percentage shot. The players should realize that if they are not able to obtain a good shot, they must maneuver and set up their teammate.

The jump shot is used almost exclusively in the Rotation since it is particularly adaptable to this type of offense. The shot is taken from approximately the same distance from the basket each time. This makes it possible to train the muscles so that the skill can be performed with more success. The shooter should always be conscious of the conditions under which he will be shooting. The shots he takes will be determined by these conditions at the time the shot is to be taken and these conditions will be the determining factor regarding its success. The player's judgment is very important and is dependent upon the conditions which exist at the time the shot is to be taken. He must look ahead far enough to anticipate the conditions as they might exist at the time of the shot and make his decisions accordingly.

The Rotation offense provides every player an opportunity to score. It utilizes the most universally used shot in basketball, the jump shot. It places a premium on shooting and emphasizes getting the high percentage shot with the belief that the better the shot, the better the chance there is of making it.

Play of the Guards and Forwards

The duties and play of the guards and forwards are similar. It is natural that the guards will be better ballhandlers and dribblers because they will be handling the ball out front more and have the responsibility of bringing the ball upcourt. The positions are interchangeable and each time a guard drives down the lane toward the basket, the opposite guard goes down the opposite side of the floor bringing the forward out to the guard position. Therefore, it is necessary that the skills and ability requirements of the guards and forwards be somewhat the same.

Play of the Center

The success of the Rotation offense can be enhanced by having a versatile center. However this is not necessary since the center can be used in various ways dependent upon his size and ability. He is, however, the key to the success of the offense in many respects whether he is used mainly as a scorer, a ballhandler, or as a screener. He is equally valuable in either capacity, but naturally it is better to have the ability to do all three.

If the center is versatile, he may be used in various ways. As a screener he must always screen facing the opponent he is screening. By so doing he can screen legally and be able to roll off his opponent after the screen and receive a pass. He must be able to move about the free throw area setting up the necessary screens whenever necessary. The center should also be in a position to receive a pass should it be necessary to pass to him. If he is a good scorer, he may be worked into the offense very effectively.

THE SCREEN

The screen is the means by which the shooter is able to get the high percentage shot. In the Rotation offense the screen is used at every opportunity. All players must be constantly aware of their responsibility to execute the screen at the proper time as part of their duty. Unless these screens are executed consistently, the offense will lose much of its effectiveness. One screen is not enough to obtain the desired shot; many times it is necessary to execute several screens before the desired shot is obtained.

The Rotation offense requires a different type of screen when the player with the ball uses it to hand off to the prospective shooter. The screen used by the players without the ball can be classified as the *orthodox* screen. Usually the screener will screen facing the man he is screening. In the Rotation the man with the ball, which in most cases is the dribbler, places his back to the player being screened out of the play and faces the player to whom he is passing the ball who, in most cases, is the shooter. By screening in this fashion the screener does not tend to be called for blocking or picking. He can see whether his team-mate is going to shoot, drive, or pass off after he receives the ball. As a result, the screener can make his next move, which will be determined by the player with the ball. If the shot is taken, the screener moves in for the rebound. If the player with the ball drives in, the screener moves in the opposite direction so that the continuity of play may be sustained and proper floor balance may be maintained. It is the constant screening and movement of all the players that makes the offense successful. The passer should always make the pass to the expected receiver unless the receiver is not in a favorable position or is unable to receive the pass. This will result in a breakdown of the continuity of play and will require a regrouping of players.

The real purpose of the screen in the Rotation is not to completely screen out an opponent but rather to delay his defensive actions to the extent that it will allow the offensive player a quick jump shot from behind the screen.

The screen is executed by placing the left foot forward if the dribbler is driving to his right or down the right side of the floor as in the front pivot. The back of the screener is toward the basket and he is facing the receiver. He establishes a wide base by spreading his feet wide apart, making it difficult for the defense to get around him. The receiver should time his movements so that when he is ready to receive the pass he will have the passer in a direct line between the basket and himself. If the shot is not attempted, the prospective shooter should take the options provided him in the continuity pattern.

Each time the dribbler drives toward the basket the guard on the opposite side of the floor moves down to the forward position and screens for the forward, both of whom have cut underneath the basket or have gone part way under and returned. Proper timing is of extreme importance and is striven for constantly.

The Rotation does not require speed. It requires timing and continuity of play and this is brought about by proper and constant screening of opponents. This does not mean that free-lance play is frowned upon, but it does mean that in a pattern offense all the players must integrate their movements or the pattern of play will break down. The Rotation demands cooperation and teamwork to insure its success.

BASIC POSITIONS

The Rotation offense requires that basic positions for each player be determined. Each player must be in the correct position before the offense can be started and continuity can be established. The guards and forwards should be able to play both positions since the duties required in each position are similar. Each player should be alert and ready to move to the nearest position open, in case a free-lance maneuver by any one player is made and the continuity of play breaks down as a result. By quickly sizing up the situation, the player can fill in the vacated position and the Rotation can continue without any delay.

The basic positions are identified in Diagram 6-1. It should be remembered that the players stationed in the areas underneath the basket should be moving back and forth underneath the basket continuously and their movements should coincide with those of the players in the guard positions.

The success of the offense depends upon the position of the players at the right time for the screen or for the shot. It is, therefore, very important that the players attempt at all times to perform the duties required of the player in the particular position he is occupying at the time. These positions are interchangeable and, if he waits his turn and performs the duty required of him, he in turn will be afforded the opportunity to shoot. In teaching the offense, either the position or areas of operation may be numbered or the players may be given numbers as is shown in the following diagrams.

SUMMARY

Basically basketball is a game of individual skills performed by players, all of whom have individual characteristics and abilities which result in their performing these skills differently. Some perform better than others and no two perform the same.

It is the coach's job, therefore, to coordinate these skills in such a manner that every player will be able to perform to the best of his ability within a framework or pattern of play which is conducive to the execution of his particular skills. This pattern should be elastic enough to allow the player to exploit his individual abilities and initiative to the utmost, yet not destroy the advantages of team play so necessary in a team game such as basketball.

All the patterns shown may be run from both sides of the floor. This, of course, helps to distribute the scoring because it is impossible for the best defensive player to always be assigned to the top scorer on the offensive team.

One of the principal advantages of the Rotation offense is that it develops a sound scoring threat. All players are able to score and use a variety of shots. In varying degrees they learn to drive, jump shoot, and rebound. Depending upon their individual abilities to react to existing conditions, the players are able to employ their particular skills at the same time during the game. An opposing team, attempting to restrain one high scorer, has the other four pitching in to take up the slack. Five all-around performers, who have been developed by a system that emphasizes equal responsibility for all players and trains players to react to the immediate problem, represent a theory that results in wins.

The Rotation tends to make the players rebound-conscious because, as the pattern unfolds and the shot is taken, each player finds himself in good rebound position at one time or another. He therefore thinks in terms of rebounding and is in position to rebound. The Rotation offense does not concede the inside rebounding position to the defense because the two back men are often in the inside position when the shot is taken and therefore have the advantage many times. The Rotation forces the defensive player to play his man in the back court, front court, and pivot positions. He must be adept at footwork and have an awareness of position. This is difficult because the Rotation tends to draw the defensive players out of their usual defensive areas, placing them at a disadvantage. They must adjust quickly to defensive changes and, more often than not, the guard may end up guarding the pivot man with whose position he is entirely unfamiliar. A good defensive guard who is a good board man may find himself on defense out front entirely away from the basket. Such mixing of offensive positions creates many defensive problems. This, of course, is what a good offensive should do.

The interchanging of post men brings about greater mobility and tends to place the burden on rear line defensive players who are unfamiliar with post defense. The alternating of men in the post position will make it virtually impossible for the post defensive man to play out in front of his man to prevent a pass-in. He must stay between his man and the basket at all times in an orthodox defensive action in order to prevent a complete collapse of the defense.

The Rotation is an offense which encourages players to use their own initiative, look for their own openings, and make their own plays. Most offenses have one or two men moving and handling the ball and the defense can set against them. In defending against the Rotation offense, the defense must move constantly in a never-ending chase. The Rotation is especially designed against the man-to-man style of play. It is built around moving screens to the inside. The center may be used in the Rotation, depending upon his ability. Usually in the basic pattern he is used as a screen and as a post man. He should be ready at all times to receive a pass from a teammate.

The Rotation gives good defensive strength against the fast break since good floor balance is maintained at all times. It also stresses teamwork and team play by all five men and, if the players are fairly proficient in excuting the fundamentals, the team will always look well coached.

In teaching the Rotation there are certain principles which must be adhered to. First, all the players must know what to do and when to do it. They must perform their assignments faultlessly; otherwise the pattern will break down and lose its continuity. Once a player understands and learns his assignments and realizes their importance in the execution of the pattern, the pattern will succeed.

Second, the players must realize that defensive strength is important at all times during all offensive maneuvers. The players should be conscious of this fact and be able to recognize any defensive weakness immediately. They must understand that defense is the responsibility of all and not just of the guards. The Rotation will place every player at one time or another in the position of being the only player between the opponents and the basket. At times such as these, the player should recognize the situation and accept the challenge and the responsibility of playing defense.

Third, the players must, while on offense, be ready to assume defensive balance if the ball changes possession, whether it be shot, dribbled, passed, or lost. Yet, they must also perform their offensive duties. This means that each player must judge quickly and accurately when he must go in for the rebound or when, being in a certain area, he must backpedal in order to prevent a fast break by the opponents.

The players should realize that no chain is stronger than its weakest link. No team is stronger than the individuals who play and practice together and who exercise a team effort to make the pattern work. This idea should be foremost in the players' minds at all times.

It should be borne in mind that the purpose of the Rotation is for the offense to force the defense back under the basket in a compact fashion. This jamming of the defense enables the offense to gain a good shooting position. If the principle of taking only good shots is stressed, the players will shoot only from set spots. The players have practiced from these spots all season.

The Rotation teaches the player to think on his own and to know when he should use his individual abilities. He knows that, if the offense is to succeed, he must accept his responsibility to his teammates because every point scored is the result of team effort. This tends to boost morale as the players see that the success of one depends upon the success of all.

The following points must be adhered to by all players if the Rotation is to operate efficiently:

1. Every man must bore in toward the basket on every exchange of the ball.
2. The ball should be handed off in an orthodox manner and it should be the same type of hand-off each time.
3. The men should stay in the areas assigned to them in order to preserve the continuity of play.
4. Every man should be watching for an opening which will allow him to drive to the basket from a reverse dribble.
5. Every man should be screen-conscious.
6. Every man should be ready to take advantage of the screen for a good percentage shot. This is the final outcome of the Rotation.
7. The post man should be ready for the pass-in at every opportunity and should screen whenever the situation demands. He sets up the offense.

8. The player who has the ball must be ready at all times to execute a pass into the post man.

The Rotation offense will produce results. Its simplicity and sound options are conducive to good scoring opportunities. It contains all the elements of a successful offense. All the needed essentials can be developed in the players with a minimum of training. The only essentials are correct timing and the proper execution of the fundamentals of basketball. These are needed in any offense.

Diagram 6-1 shows the predetermined position of all five players. Their positions will remain fundamentally the same with the players moving into areas occupied by other players and other players moving into areas previously occupied by them. The forwards and guards No. 1, 2, 3, and 4 will move in a complete circle under the basket and out around the free throw circle area in a continuous movement. The No. 3 forward will move in the circle in direct opposition to forward No. 4. No. 1 guard will move in direct opposition to No. 2 guard. The guard going down the left side of the free throw lane will move in direct opposition to the forward on the same side of the floor or he will be continuing the circle in the opposite direction. All four players therefore move in a complete circle excepting when the continuity is broken by a player reversing his direction or free-lancing. If the player does change direction, this means that all players must do likewise and do so immediately in order to continue the continuity of play.

DIAGRAM 6-1

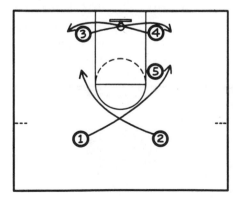

Diagram 6-2 shows the area from which the majority of shots will be taken if the offense is executed properly. It can be readily seen that the defense must be forced back toward the basket so that 15 to 18 foot jump shots may be obtained from behind the screen. This means that every player must execute his duties perfectly and must be screen conscious at all times. This will jam the defense and enable the offensive players to obtain good shooting position. The players must adhere to this theory at all times if the offense is to be successful. Although the diagram shows that all shots are taken from outcourt, this is not necessarily true because it is possible, by reversing direction, for the dribbler to catch his guard overplaying him and drive in for a layup. It is possible also for the center to score close in. It should also be remembered that the outcourt shots are all taken from behind the screen.

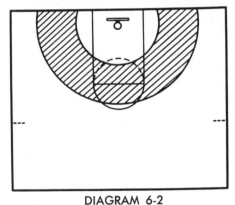

DIAGRAM 6-2

Diagram 6-3 shows the beginning of the pattern with player No. 1 driving to his right. No. 5 can move up or stay stationary with No. 1 using him as a screen. If No. 5's guard does not switch and pick up

DIAGRAM 6-3

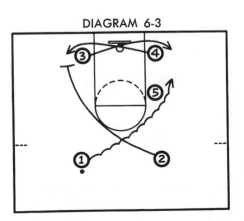

No. 1 after the screen No. 1 can execute a jump shot. No. 1 should try and move as close to No. 5 as possible and use No. 5 as a screen. No. 3 and No. 4 cross underneath the basket. No. 2 moves down the opposite side of the free throw lane and screens for No. 4 who has cut underneath the basket. The guards should maneuver out front so that the proper angle for the drive-in can be attained. The success of this initial movement depends to a great extent upon No. 1's ability to free himself using No. 5 as a screen. No. 1 and No. 2's guards will have a tendency to play to the outside, thereby making it difficult for the dribbler to stay in close enough to effectively use No. 5 as a screen unless, of course, No. 5 moves out further to the side and then gradually moves in as the rotation of the players continues. This situation is not desirable and should be avoided if possible by having the two guards work together and try and get the right angle for the driving dribble. This can be done by proper maneuvering and reversing direction or by allowing the guards to drive down the middle if the defense plays them to far to the outside. Also, it is possible for the guard without the ball to exchange positions with one of the forwards thereby preventing a switch of the defense out front. It is important for the players underneath the basket to stay close to the free throw lane and not venture outcourt too far or it will be difficult to change positions underneath and obtain proper timing.

Diagram 6-4 shows the same general set-up except that No. 2 has the ball and drives to his left. If he cannot drive all the way in, he passes to No. 1 who has faked to his left and then cut to his right, receiving a pass from No. 2 who has stopped and pivoted so that he can make the pass to No. 1. After receiving the pass, No. 1 continues to his right, driving hard toward No. 5 and down the right side of the lane. He attempts to use No. 5 as a screen to brush off his guard. If this is accomplished, No. 1 may execute a jump shot from this position near the

DIAGRAM 6-4

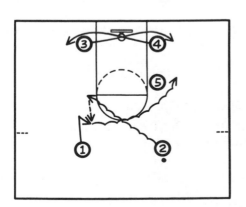

circle. It is important that the guards work together very closely in order that the initial movements of the players may be instigated. This maneuver is just one of the many that can be used by the guards in order to start the preliminary moves of the offense. Much depends upon the ingenuity of the guards and, as shown in the previous diagram, if the defensive forward overplays the dribbler, the offensive player should move immediately to the inside. If the guards maneuver correctly, it will force the defensive forwards to shift. As the guards maneuver it should be remembered that the main object is to get an angle on the defensive forward so that the dribbler is able to force his opponent into the post man for the screen. The guards should try to avoid being forced too far to the outside. They should work and practice together a great deal in order to obtain the proper timing.

Diagram 6-5 shows a continuation of the rotation, providing the maneuvers shown in the previous diagrams do not result in a scoring opportunity. No. 1 continues his drive toward the basket and down the free throw lane bearing in toward the lane as much as possible and as far as possible. He should try to be as close to the preferred shooting area as possible when he stops his dribble. As No. 1 approaches the area (as

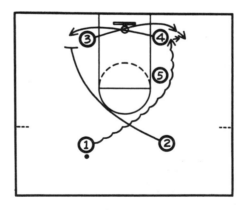

DIAGRAM 6-5

shown in the diagram) and sees that he cannot go all the way in for the layup, he stops his dribble and executes a front pivot (placing the left foot forward and toward the end line) so that his back is toward the basket. No. 3 in the meantime has exchanged positions with No. 4 from whom he receives a screen while crossing underneath the basket. He times his

cut so that he arrives at the desired position which is directly in front
of No. 1 at the time No. 1 is ready to pass the ball to him. After No. 1 stops
his dribble, he passes to and screens for No. 3, who executes a jump shot
from this position. No. 1 should provide as good a screen as possible by
spreading his feet wide thereby making it difficult for the defense. When
No. 1 drives for the basket the opposite guard No. 2 always goes down
the opposite side of the free throw lane for the screen on the forward.
The forward will come out to the guard position.

Diagram 6-6 shows No. 3 in the desired position for a high percentage shot. No. 1 passes him the ball using the prescribed two-hand
underhand pass. The cuts underneath the basket should be timed so that
No. 3 will arrive at the opportune time for the pass off from No. 1. The
success of the play will depend to a large extent on the maneuvers of
No. 3 and No. 4 underneath the basket. The shot from this position is
one of the most successful shots in the Rotation offense providing the
play is executed properly. It is the really first indication of rotating the
players. No. 3 should time his cut so that he will be at the desired spot
at exactly the proper moment, that moment being just as No. 1 stops his
dribble, pivots and is ready to pass off to No. 3. In the meantime action
has resulted on the opposite side of the floor. No. 2 has screened for No. 4
who either times his cut underneath the basket so that No. 2 will be able
to execute a moving screen or remains stationary outside and close to
the free throw lane thereby enabling No. 2 to screen off for him. He also
can help free himself and make it difficult for his guard to stay with him
by faking a cut underneath the basket, trying to take his guard with him
for a couple of steps and then reversing his drive at about the same time
No. 2 is attempting to set a screen for him. No. 4 should cut to the outside

DIAGRAM 6-6

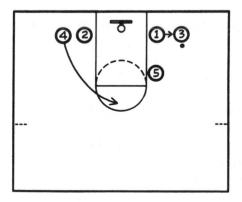

of No. 2 so that No. 2 can effectively execute his screen on No. 4's guard who will be playing him to the inside.

Diagram 6-7 shows that No. 3 now has three options if he is not able to shoot directly off the screen provided him by No. 1. His guard will be behind No. 1 if the cut and screen is executed properly. If his guard goes to the left of No. 1 in an attempt to block No. 3's shot, No. 3 may take one dribble to his left and get the jump shot. If his guard goes to the right, No. 3 may take the dribble to his right and get the shot. No. 3 may also

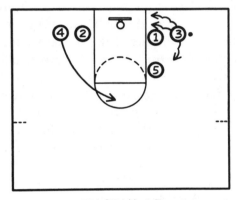

DIAGRAM 6-7

drive the baseline if his guard goes behind No. 1 in an attempt to cut off the drive out. The pattern of play at this point will depend upon the action of No. 3 and his decision of what to do. The other players' maneuvers will depend upon that decision. No. 2 has already driven down the opposite side of the free throw lane with the expectation that No. 4 will, after a screen from No. 2, drive out toward the free throw circle area. No. 4 needs to time this movement and if No. 3 is having difficulty or is undecided as to what to do in regard to his three options, No. 4 may return to his position underneath the basket and screen for No. 2 whose position he has taken. If, on the other hand, No. 3 is in danger of being tied up, No. 4 will take the right guard position bringing No. 2 out to the other guard position and No. 1, cutting underneath the basket so that proper floor balance is maintained and the rotation may proceed with a minimum of delay. This is a situation whereby floor balance can be accomplished very quickly without undue delay as every player should be able to move to any position other than the pivot and perform the function or maneuver required of him. The players should learn to move into the correct positions automatically and without hesitation.

Diagram 6-8 shows that, should No. 3 decide to drive out toward the guard position because he is unable to get the high percentage shot, he will receive a screen from No. 5 enabling him to drive to his right toward the guard position but also in a circle toward the free throw line area. No. 2 in the meantime has driven down the opposite and left side of the lane and executed a screen for No. 4 who has cut underneath the basket exchanging positions with No. 3. No. 4 now drives out toward the guard position in an attempt to meet No. 3. This should take place approximately at the free throw line area directly in front of the basket. No. 3 will stop his dribble, execute a front pivot with the right foot forward and his back to the basket. No. 4 now is directly in front of No. 3 and receives a pass from No. 3. No. 4 now has the opportunity of the 15 to 18 foot jump shot from behind the screen. Timing is important here and No. 4 must do one of three things so that this timing may be accomplished and his drive to meet No. 3 will be consumated at precisely the right time. No. 4 may time his cut underneath the basket so that he will be able to make his cut at the precise moment to enable him to meet No. 3 and at the same time take advantage of the screen provided him by No. 2. He may also, as indicated in the previous diagram, fake a cut underneath the basket, going part way underneath and come back out in time to meet No. 3 as indicated or he may remain stationary close to the free throw lane, take advantage of the screen and make his cut when he sees No. 3 is approximately in the correct position.

DIAGRAM 6-8

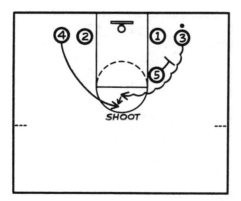

Diagram 6-9 shows that, should No. 4 be unable to get the shot off, he can continue the drive to his right down the right side of the free throw lane receiving a screen from No. 5 until he meets No. 2 who has cut underneath the basket and exchanged positions with No. 1. No. 2 should time his cut underneath the basket in such a way that he arrives at the desired position at the same time No. 4 arrives at his. No. 4 stops his dribble and executes a front pivot placing his left foot forward and toward the end line. This will place his back to the basket and leave him in a position to screen for No. 2. No. 4 should assume a wide base and remember that the screen should be set with his back to the basket and facing the sideline with the left leg toward the end line. No. 3, after passing to No. 4, holds his screen until No. 4 makes his commitment as to whether he will shoot or continue the rotation. If he decides to shoot, No. 3 goes in for the rebound. If No. 4 decides to dribble to his right, No. 3 will cut down the left side of the free throw lane and set a screen for No. 1 who has cut underneath the basket exchanging positions with No. 2. No. 1 and No. 2 will wait for the exchange of position which, of course, will be accompanied by the appropriate screen until they can anticipate that No. 4 will be in the correct position so that No. 2 will be able to meet him at precisely the right time for the pass from No. 4 and the high percentage shot. It should be mentioned here that No. 1 and No. 2 may exchange positions constantly underneath the basket during the maneuvering of the players out front in an effort to confuse or gain

DIAGRAM 6-9

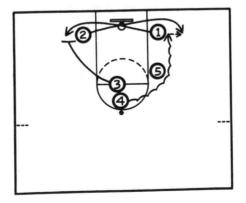

an advantage over their guards, but while doing this, care should be taken that they are in the correct position to make the cut to receive the pass when they are expected to.

Diagram 6-10 shows No. 2, instead of continuing the rotation (perhaps because he has been forced too far out to the sideline or his guard has him blocked off) passing the ball to No. 5. No. 2 then cuts in front of No. 5 and receives a pass from him. No. 2 dribbles across the free throw lane with No. 5 screening for him. No. 2 drives in for a layup if possible. If this is not possible, he drives as far as possible and meets No. 1 who has crossed under the basket exchanging positions with No. 2. No. 1 and No. 2 should collaborate so that the screen and timing of the cut will free No. 1 for the desired shot. Here again the success of the maneuver depends to a large extent upon the correct maneuvering under the basket and the advantage No. 1 takes of the screen afforded him by No. 3. If No. 1 takes the shot No. 2 goes in for the rebound as does No. 4, 3, and 5. If No. 1 decides to continue the rotation, he does so by dribbling in the same direction from whence he came and down the right side of the free

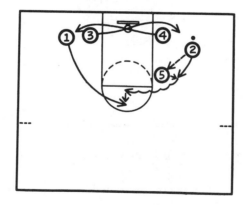

DIAGRAM 6-10

throw lane. When he turns down the shot and continues the rotation, this immediately signals the other players to assume their proper positions for continuation of the rotation. This means that No. 5 will stay on the same side of the free throw lane and No. 3 and No. 4 will assume the proper positions along the outside of the free throw lane underneath the basket in preparation for the exchange of position and proper movement underneath. No. 2 remains in the vicinity of the free throw area to defend against the fast break by the opposition should they gain possession of the ball from the rebound. This situation of having No. 2 stay back will apply to No. 1, 3, or No. 4 should they be in a similar position after a shot is taken.

Diagram 6-11 is an option play from Diagram 6-9 and shows No. 2 cutting past No. 5 after having passed the ball to him. After the cut has been made by No. 2, No. 5 who still has possession of the ball, fakes to his left and dribbles to his right across the free throw area, keeping his body between the ball and his opponent. No. 2 continues across the free throw lane and down the left side. In doing so he screens for No. 1 who cuts toward the guard position. No. 1 should time his maneuver to receive the pass from No. 5 at the proper time to assure himself of a good percentage shot. No. 1 and No. 4 have previously crossed underneath the basket and stationed themselves in the correct position for a continuation

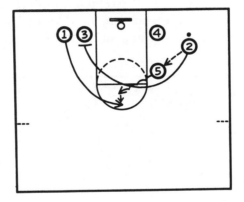

DIAGRAM 6-11

of the rotation. If No. 1 expects a screen from No. 3 he must attempt to place himself in an advantageous position for such a screen. He can do this by being in the right place at the right time so that No. 3 can follow his particular assignment and by so doing can execute the screen with efficiency. No. 1 does not need to stand stationary but can time his movements so that he can be at the particular spot at the correct time by anticipating the movements of all the other players and particularly Nos. 3 and 5. If at any time any player finds himself out of position he should immediately attempt to establish proper floor balance by quickly going to the proper position in relation to the positions occupied by his teammates.

Diagram 6-12 shows an option to Diagrams 6-7 and 6-8. No. 3 passes the ball to No. 5 and makes the cut. No. 5 fakes to his right and after No. 3 has made his cut, then dribbles to his left bearing in toward the basket and keeping his body between the ball and his opponent. No. 2, seeing that No. 3 does not receive the pass, cuts underneath the basket exchanging positions with No. 1. No. 1 should screen for No. 2 as he cuts underneath the basket and the maneuver should be timed so that No. 2 will be free to receive a pass off from No. 5 when No. 5 is in the correct position to make the pass. No. 3 continues down the left side of the lane and screens for No. 4, who cuts out toward the guard position so that he can be in a position to continue the rotation should No. 2 decide not to shoot. This maneuver will require constant shifting of the defensive personnel because the swift interchanging of positions along with the screens which have been executed will make it virtually impossible for the defensive players

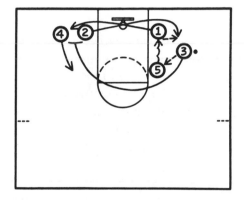

DIAGRAM 6-12

to play a strict man to man style of play. No. 5, of course, should be prepared to shoot if he has a good opportunity to do so before he passes off to No. 2. This, of course, will be dependent upon factors which he will need to make a decision about at the moment. It should always be remembered that the entire rotation may be reversed by the dribbler should he desire to do so. The best time to do this is when the dribbler has the ball out front or near the free throw circle area. If the rotation is reversed it means that the screener goes back the same direction from whence he came and all other players reverse direction.

Diagram 6-13 shows a situation where the opposition are forcing the offensive guards too far to the sides to enable either to start the drive in

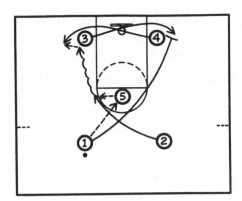

DIAGRAM 6-13

toward the basket. If this is done, No. 1 passes the ball to No. 5 who has assumed a position at the high post. No. 1 makes the cut past No. 5 but does not receive the ball. He continues down the right side of the lane and screens for No. 3 who has exchanged positions with No. 4. No. 2 cuts behind No. 1 and receives a pass from No. 5. If No. 2 is not able to execute the jump shot after having received the pass from No. 5, he continues his dribble down the left side of the lane either for a layup or to meet No. 4 who has exchanged positions with No. 3. If the timing appears to be too difficult for Nos. 3 and 4, and No. 3 sees that it will be impossible to meet No. 2 in the correct position for a good percentage shot, he may break part way under the basket and return to his original position as does No. 4. There should be perfect understanding between the players cutting under the basket because this is the key to the success of the maneuver.

Diagram 6-14 shows a variation in the preceding diagram. No. 1 passes the ball to No. 5 at the high post and makes his cut past No. 5 as does No. 2. Instead of giving the ball to No. 2, No. 5 keeps it and dribbles to his left or to the opposite side of the last cutter. He should protect the ball by keeping his body between it and his guard. No. 5 does not drive toward the basket with the idea of scoring unless his guard switches to one of the cutters and he is left open. He should dribble down the right side of the free throw lane with the idea that he will meet No. 3 who will have cut underneath the basket exchanging positions with No. 4. No. 3 will time his cut so that he will meet No. 5 in the position shown in the diagram. No. 5 will stop his dribble with his back to the basket and hand off the ball to No. 3 who is in a position for the shot from behind the screen afforded by No. 5. If No. 5's guard switches, No. 3 will take one bounce to either the right or left of No. 5 depending upon which side of No. 5 the guard has committed himself to, and then be in a posi-

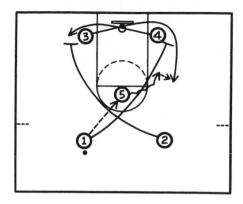

DIAGRAM 6-14

tion to get his shot away. In all instances it is left up to the good judgment of the shooter to determine whether he has a good shot. He should think ahead at all times. No. 1 will screen for No. 3 and No. 2 will screen for No. 4.

Diagram 6-15 shows the continuity of play if No. 3 decides not to shoot. This decision must be made a split second before the shooter receives the ball. He will not have time to make a decision after he receives the ball. The diagram shows No. 3 continuing in the same path from whence he came. He continues the dribble to his right across the free throw area with the intention of meeting No. 4 who has cut underneath the basket and is coming out toward the guard position with the express

DIAGRAM 6-15

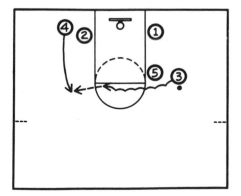

purpose, after having obtained a screen from No. 2, of meeting with No. 3. No. 3 protects the ball with his body during the dribble and, at the opportune time, stops and pivots with his back to the basket; and facing No. 4, he hands off to No. 4 who is now in a position where he can shoot from behind the screen provided by No. 3. No. 5 immediately shifts to the side of the free throw lane and prepares to screen for his teammates as the rotation continues. It should be borne in mind that No. 3 may reverse his direction at any time if his guard overplays him. If this is done, all other players will do likewise so that the floor balance is maintained.

7

The Shuffle Offense

Bruce Drake, the famed coach of the University of Oklahoma, Norman, Oklahoma, was the innovator of the Shuffle offense. He developed the offense in an effort to find one that could readily be adapted to any defense or situation. Several professional articles by Coach Drake appeared early in coaching magazines explaining the offense, and by 1952 it was famous enough that he was highly in demand at coaching clinics throughout the nation to explain and lecture on its intricacies and its patterns. To say that it was a success would be the understatement of the basketball age. It became the "rave" of the basketball world. Joel Eaves, who at that time was the basketball coach at Auburn University, wrote a complete book about the offense entitled *Basketball's Shuffle Offense.* This book came off the press of Prentice-Hall, Inc. in 1960 and was highly effective in popularizing the offense to a greater extent because of the complete coverage it gave to the offense.

In 1952, when lecturing at clinics, Bruce Drake made the statement that he believed he finally had the one offense that could be used against all defenses. He asked anyone who discovered a way to improve the offense to please inform him since he was constantly working toward this end. Since that time he has had plenty of help. Books, plus hundreds of professional articles published in professional journals have been written about the Shuffle offense. Today, almost any professional coaching magazine will feature an article explaining some phase or some new application of the offense. The Shuffle has been applied to every formation in basketball. The offense was used extensively throughout the southern sections of the United States at first, but now is in use practically everywhere basketball is played. Many coaches feel that it is the greatest offense ever devised that can be used against a man-to-man defense, claiming that it utterly destroys this defense, and that it drives opponents to the use of zone defenses in retaliation. Drake devised it with the hope that it would riddle *both* defenses. One famous coach from a southern state stated while lecturing on the Shuffle offense, "This offense has 34,000 different options." Whether he had actually counted this many options in the offense is doubtful, but the statement does illustrate the potential it has and the many scoring opportunities it presents.

It is not the purpose of this chapter to present all the potentialities of the Shuffle offense, but rather to give the basic ideas regarding the offense. This will enable the coach to make his own application of the offensive maneuvers presented to his particular situation and material.

The Shuffle offense has three basic movements. They are (1) the change of sides, (2) the "solo game," and (3) the rolling game. These basic movements are not separate offenses, but are options to the same offense to give it more effectiveness in overcoming certain defensive maneuvers that might be employed against it, or to stop certain phases of it. The different basic movements are therefore used to counter different defensive reactions to the offense.

The Change of Sides

The basic positions of the offense are shown in Diagram 7-1 and are numbered from one to five. If the offense starts with an overload to the left, the players would start in the numbered positions as shown. After executing one movement or change of sides, the players would end up in the shadowed positions shown on the opposite (in this case the right) side. Since the players continually change positions and must play all positions as the movement continues, it is important to remember the numbered positions on the floor. The *number 1* position with the overload to the left is low along the right side of the free throw lane. This player works this area for openings and for the change of sides movement to begin the ball must be passed to him as low and as near to the free throw lane as possible. This is the only forcing pass in the offense, and ways of substituting and maneuvering for this forcing pass will be shown later.

The *number 2* position is in the center of the floor, and nearer the midcourt line than the *number 3* position. It is the one position that

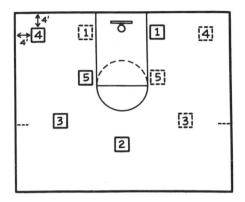

DIAGRAM 7-1

never changes, always being straight out from the basket and in the center of the court at the top of the free throw circle.

The *number 3* position should be a split position between the *number 4* and *5* positions. It should be nearer the basket and end line than the *number 2* position. The ball should be brought down to this position most of the time and usually the player in this position triggers the movement that starts the offense. The player in the *number 4* position plays or starts play about one and one-half steps from the end line and the same distance from the sideline or about four feet in each situation. The *number 5* position is at the side of the foul line and outside the free throw lane. In showing the movements of the players in the "change of sides" maneuver, the numbered positions on the floor will be maintained to show how the players move to each position in the continuity of the pattern.

Diagram 7-2 shows the basic "change of side" movement. No. 3 passes the ball to No. 2. When this pass is being made, or as it is being made, No. 1 feints toward the lane and the baseline and then comes back out to get the pass from No. 2. This pass should be as low and near the free throw lane as possible. As the pass is made from No. 3 to No. 2, No. 4 moves to the baseline. No. 3 now becomes the first cutter. He breaks down and then cuts either over or behind No. 5 as shown in the diagram with a burst of speed and change of pace. He could be open for a nice drop pass from No. 1, but if not, he continues on across to the opposite side of the floor and to the *number 4* position. After receiving the ball from No. 2, No. 1 dribbles out to the *number 3* spot on the right side of the floor, but he watches for openings and for scoring opportunities as he does so. No. 4 now breaks out to the No. 5 position from the base-line and could be open. After passing to No. 1, No. 2 waits briefly until No. 3 cuts by No. 5. He then screens for No. 5 and continues on into the weak-side or the new *number 1* position on the left side of the floor. No. 5 first screens for No. 3 (he may move out to do this), then fakes a move toward the basket and then comes back up in a movement off the screen set by No. 2 as he moved in. No. 5 may be open as a result of this ma-neuver, but if not he continues on out to the top of the circle and into the *number 2* position.

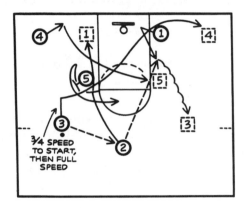

DIAGRAM 7-2

DIAGRAM 7-3

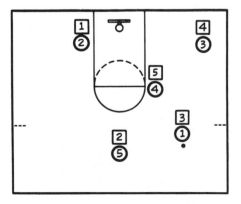

The numbered players in Diagram 7-2, after a change of sides, are now in an overload to the right and in the numbered positions shown in Diagram 7-3. No. 1 has the ball in the *number 3* position. No. 3 is now in the *number 4* position; No. 5 is in the *number 2* position; No. 4 is in the *number 5* position and No. 2 is in the *number 1* position.

Keeping in mind the player numbers as they began in Diagram 7-2, they are now positioned as shown in Diagram 7-4 and are about to execute a new change-of-side movement and a change in positions again. Diagram 7-4 shows the continuity of the pattern and how the players change positions in the pattern and in changing the overload from side to side. No. 1 passes to No. 5 and cuts by No. 4 and goes to the *number 4* position. No. 5 passes to No. 2 and after screening for No. 4, goes to the *number 1* position. No. 4 comes back off No. 5's screen and back out to the *number 2* position. No. 3 breaks into the *number 5* position and No. 2 dribbles out to the *number 3* position. The change-of-side movement could continue indefinitely, but probably never would do so, except as the coach would use it to teach the individual player movements in the offense. There will be many scoring opportunities which will arise as a result of the movements in the "change of sides." However, the change in the positions by the players give every player a chance to play the different positions and this requires a team whose members are versatile enough to play all the positions. If the team should execute the "change of side" movement five times, the players would have rotated their positions once and, as a result, would be back in their original starting positions, but they would be positioned in an overload to the opposite side of the floor from which they began the first movement.

DIAGRAM 7-4

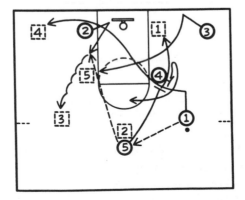

The Shuffle offense is in reality a free-lance game, yet one that has a continuity pattern that can use set plays and be considered as a disciplined offense. It can be changed to meet various situations as the need arises. If the team has one big pivot player and it is to the best advantage to keep him in the pivot spot rather than rotate him in the other positions, this can easily be done as shown in Diagram 7-5. The "change of sides" move is shown in this diagram. The pass goes from No. 3 to No. 2 to No. 1, with No. 3 cutting by the pivot man No. 5. No. 5, instead of swinging off the screen provided him by No. 2 out to the *number 2* position, swings across the lane to take the pivot-post position there. No. 4, instead of breaking from the baseline up into the *number 5* position, breaks out to the *number 2* position and now with No. 5, the big pivot man staying in the pivot-post position at all times, the continuity of the Shuffle continues with the other players rotating in the positions and using the pattern shown.

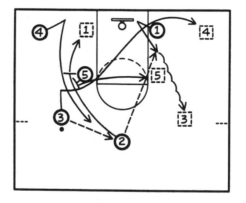

DIAGRAM 7-5

Offensive rebounding responsibilities must definitely be established. Drills must be used until the rebounding duties become automatic. As an example, if a shot should be taken from the *number 3* area (see Diagram 7-6), the players in the *1, 4,* and *5* positions would cover the rebounding positions shown. If No. 1 should recover the rebound, he could clear the ball out to the side and the players could shift as shown in the diagram and be ready to set the offense up again. If the rebound should go off to the other side, they are already set up to begin the offense.

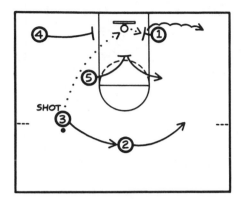

DIAGRAM 7-6

Diagram 7-7 shows the offense throwing three and one-half men on the offensive board. If the ball comes out to the right, they fill the positions shown with No. 3, or the player in the *number 3* position always going to the *number 3* position on the opposite side of the floor. The players must be well drilled in covering rebounding responsibilities.

DIAGRAM 7-7

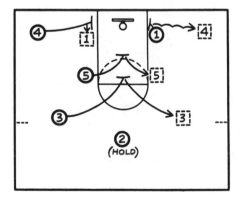

If the offense wishes to throw four offensive men on the board for rebounding, they would do it as shown in Diagram 7-8. The player in the *number 2* position would stay in this position for defensive balance.

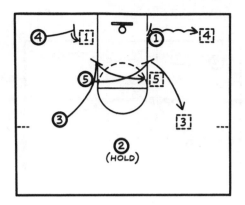

DIAGRAM 7-8

At times in an offensive situation, the team may want to throw five men on the offensive board for rebounds. The five men would cover in the Shuffle offense as shown in Diagram 7-9. If they should recover the ball to the right, they would cover the positions as shown in the diagram.

DIAGRAM 7-9

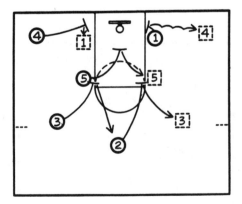

The Solo Game

In order to run the "change of sides" pattern, there is one forcing pass that must be made to "trigger" this movement. The ball must move from No. 3 to No. 2 to No. 1. The real forcing pass is the one from *the number 2 to the number 1* position. If this pass cannot be made, the offense cannot function properly. Naturally, after the "change of sides" has been worked a few times, the defense will put pressure at the vital points to prevent this maneuver. Since the player in the *number 3* position is usually the "triggerman" or quarterback for the offense, the first defensive pressure will come on the pass from No. 3 to No. 2 and then more pressure to prevent the pass from No. 2 to No. 1. The shadowed areas in Diagram 7-10 show the area where the defense will pressure, over-play, and overshift to prevent the passes and to force the offense into unnatural positions that will throw the timing of the offense off. No offense should have to rely on one forcing pass to function effectively. When the defense pressures at these points, the offense can use the "solo game." In actuality the "solo game" is a free-lance game that the team uses until such time as the pass can be made from the *number 2* position to the *number 1* position thereby initiating the beginning of the change-of-side movement. In the "solo game" the players pass and cut, filling the floor positions as needed, but still keeping the basic formation.

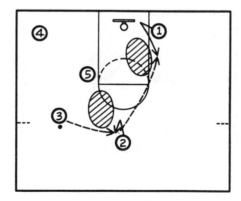

DIAGRAM 7-10

Diagram 7-11 shows the player in the *number 3* position passing to No. 4 and cutting past No. 5 for a possible opening. The timing of No. 3's

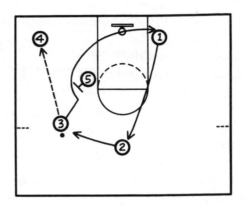

DIAGRAM 7-11

cut is important in this move. His best move is probably to maneuver slowly at first and then give a burst of speed by the screen set by No. 5. If he is open, No. 4 can pass to him. When no opening occurs, the players fill the position as shown with No. 3 going to the *number 1* position. No. 1 goes to the *number 2* position and No. 2 goes to the *number 3* position. They are now ready to continue the offense.

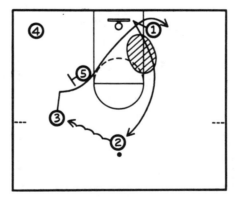

DIAGRAM 7-12

Diagram 7-12 shows a continuation of the "solo game." No. 3 has passed to No. 2. The defensive pressure as shown in the shadowed area has prevented No. 2 from passing to No. 1 immediately, so the "solo cut" is used. No. 3 now cuts in front of or behind No. 5 to get open. He may take a pass from No. 2 if open. If no opening occurs, then No. 2 dribbles over and fills the *number 3* position. No. 3 fills the *number 1* position and No. 1 fills the *number 2* position coming out to the top of the circle to do so.

If the defense is pressuring the pass to the player in the *number 2* position, the first thing to do is to have No. 1 and No. 2 exchange positions as shown in Diagram 7-13. As soon as No. 2 realizes there is pressure being brought to bear, he should move in to screen for No. 1. No. 1 should come out from behind the screen and should be free as he moves up to the *number 2* position to receive a pass from No. 3. He might be open for a pass or shot in a deeper position than shown in the diagram. As he receives the ball in the *number 2* position, and as a result of the movement and shake up of the defense, he can now relay the ball to the *number 1* position and the "change of sides" movement can begin.

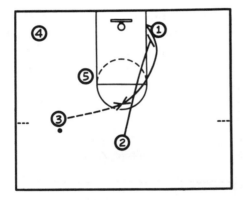

DIAGRAM 7-13

The "solo game" in which free-lance moves are used can result in many scoring opportunities. In Diagram 7-14 No. 3 passes to No. 4 and then breaks by No. 5 for a possible opening. After No. 3 moves by No. 5, No. 5 maneuvers to a lower pivot-post position. At the same time No. 4 makes an adjustment dribble and passes the ball into No. 5 in a pivot-post maneuver. No. 4 follows his pass for a possible opening in a drive to the basket.

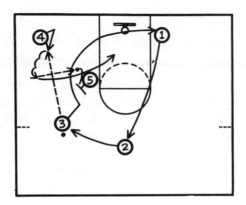

DIAGRAM 7-14

If, as shown in Diagram 7-14, No. 4 was not open in his cut by No. 5 in the pivot-post position, the players again fill the positions as shown in Diagram 7-15. No. 4 moves into the *number 1* position. No. 1 moves to the *number 2* position, No. 2 moves to the *number 3* position, and No. 3 moves to the *number 4* position. Variations in filling the different positions could be worked out so that it fits the team personnel better. For instance, in this play No. 4 could hook back to his left and return to his original position and Nos. 1, 2, and 3 could remain in their positions which they had just filled after the cut made by No. 3 in the play shown in Diagram 7-14.

DIAGRAM 7-15

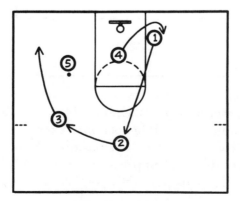

If the defensive player covering No. 3 decides to anticipate his cut past No. 5 and waits for him behind No. 5 with the intent of picking him up at this point or of preventing any pass to him after he cuts by No. 5, then No. 3 should use the maneuver as shown in Diagram 7-16. The illustration shows No. 3 passing to No. 2, faking a drive past No. 5 and then stepping back as No. 4 and No. 5 set a double screen. As No. 3 steps back from his fake drive, No. 2 passes him the ball. No. 3 can shoot or pass to No. 1. If the ball goes to No. 1, the "change of sides" maneuver can be initiated.

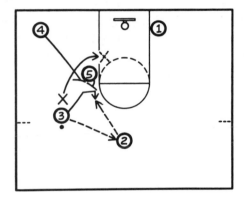

DIAGRAM 7-16

DIAGRAM 7-17

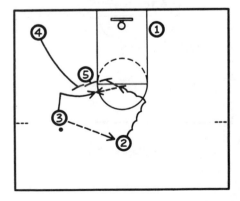

Diagram 7-17 shows a three-man screen being set for an easy shot for No. 3. In executing this maneuver No. 3 passes to No. 2 and No. 2, not being able to pass to No. 1, starts a dribble in toward the basket. No. 5 and No. 4 position themselves as shown in the diagram. No. 2 dribbles the ball toward them, flips it to No. 3 who has faked a cut past No. 5, then steps back for the pass from No. 2 and an easy shot.

The Rolling Game

There will be times when the defense will sag or collapse to stop this offense, gambling on the outside shot not being effective. The answer to the collapsing defense is the "rolling game." The "rolling game" is a dribbling offense and with it the defense can be pressed in close to the basket area for shots. It will also provide free-lance maneuvers which will result in scoring opportunities. It can also be combined with the "solo game" and like the "solo game," can be used until the ball is moved to the *number 1* position and the starting position for the "change of sides" maneuvers.

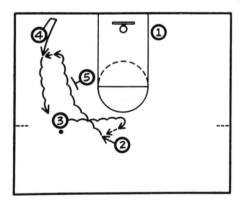

DIAGRAM 7-18

Remember in Diagram 7-13 in explaining the "solo game," it was mentioned that if the defense pressured the pass to No. 2, the first thing to do was to execute an exchange of positions between the *number 1* and *number 2* positions. The second thing to do if this pressure is intense is to go into the "rolling game." To do this, No. 3 dribbles to the inside of No. 2 and hands off to No. 2, as shown in Diagram 7-18. No. 2 drives with the dribble as shown and hands off to No. 4. The positions are now filled again. It should be remembered that anytime the ball goes to the *number 2* position, No. 4 cuts to the baseline and is ready to break out to the *number 5* position on the opposite side of the floor. The *number 3* position is anywhere between the *number 2* and *number 4* position. Anytime that No. 3 dribbles toward No. 2, No. 5 should play out opposite the free throw line and possibly move out to create more screening possibilities for the dribblers on the play. Also, when No. 3 dribbles toward No. 2, the player in the *number 2* position should hold his position until No. 3 has almost reached him before he cuts or breaks by No. 3 to receive the ball.

While the "rolling game" is a dribbling maneuver, it is for the purpose of scoring or to manipulate the defense so that the "forcing pass" to No. 1 can be made. When this pass is made, the "change of sides" is begun. After dribbling over to the *number 2* position, as shown in Diagram 7-19, No. 3 suddenly passes the ball into No. 1 and now the players go into the "change of sides" move as shown and begin looking for all the scoring opportunities that are possible from the play.

DIAGRAM 7-19

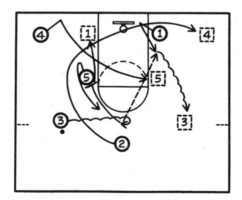

The "rolling game" and the "solo game" can be combined at times by just filling the positions as shown in Diagram 7-20. No. 3 dribbles toward the *number 2* position and just as the exchange is about to occur, No. 3 passes to No. 5 on the pivot-post position. No. 2 now swings out and around No. 3 making the cut through as if he were coming from the *number 3* position. If No. 2 is not open, he moves into the *number 1* position. No. 3 follows his pass to No. 5 and receives a pass from him. If, however, he is not open for a shot he goes into the "rolling game" again, dribbling toward No. 4 and handing off to him. No. 4 dribbles out to the *number 3* position. No. 1 moves out to the *number 2* position and the positions are all filled again.

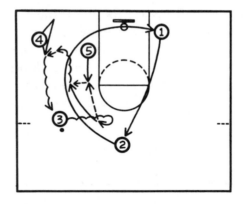

DIAGRAM 7-20

The "rolling game" moves easily into the "change of sides" as shown in Diagram 7-21. No. 3 dribbles in toward No. 4, who fakes toward the baseline and then, as No. 3 almost reaches the *number 4* position, No. 4 comes out to take a hand-off from No. 3. No. 4 now dribbles out to the *number 3* position in an exchange maneuver. From the *number 3* position No. 4 dribbles toward No. 2 and No. 2 holds until the dribble is almost there before breaking over for a hand-off. As No. 2 breaks toward the dribbler, the dribbler who was No. 4 in the beginning, instead of handing off to No. 2, turns and passes the ball into No. 1. The "change of sides" maneuver is now in operation. No. 2 moves out and makes the cut from the *number 3* position past No. 5. The positions are now filled

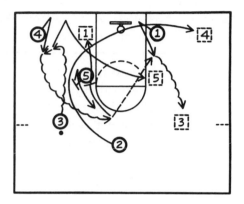

DIAGRAM 7-21

DIAGRAM 7-22

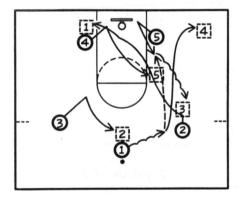

as usual with the scoring opportunities being taken as they become available in this versatile offense.

Other Variations in the Shuffle

The Shuffle offense can be started or begun from almost any formation. Diagram 7-22 shows the offense being started from the three-out and two-in formation, with the ball being passed into No. 5 which would be the equivalent of a pass into the *number 1* position. The offense shifts into the overload formation by filling the various positions as shown in the diagram. The pass could have gone to No. 5 from No. 2, whereby the shifting of positions would have been the same.

It is very easy to shift the offense from one side of the floor to the other. Diagram 7-23 shows the overload shifted to the left; however, it can be quickly shifted to the right side by the move shown here. No. 3 passes to No. 2 and No. 2 dribbles over to the *number 3* position on the right side of the floor and the other players fill the positions to the right as shown in the diagram.

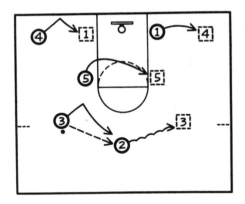

DIAGRAM 7-23

Against a Zone Defense

Diagram 7-24 shows how, with very little adjustment, this offense will operate effectively against zone defenses. The offense is set up in an overload formation to one side of the floor or another. The diagram shows the overload shift. The possible movements from the *number 1* position can make the adjustments in the overshift as needed. The first possibility against a zone is the use of the "solo game." The offense can move into the "solo game" and, as a result of the individual "solo cuts," into overload situations. Many scoring opportunities will be obtained.

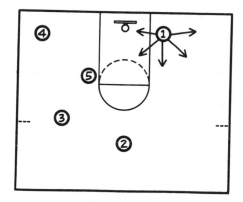

DIAGRAM 7-24

The solo game results in greater player movement which is necessary against the zone and with rapid movement of the ball many scoring plays will result.

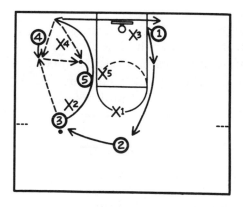

DIAGRAM 7-25

Diagram 7-25 shows a possible overload situation. No. 3 passes to No. 4 and cuts around No. 5 to the baseline where a passing triangle is formed for an exchange between Nos. 4, 3, and 5 for possible scoring opportunities. If none are in evidence, No. 3 fills the *number 1* position, No. 2 moves to the *number 3* position, and No. 1 moves to the *number 2* position. Many other passing combinations are possible from this formation such as a pass from No. 5 to No. 2 to No. 1, which will result in good scoring possibilities.

Diagram 7-26 shows the movement and passing maneuvers against the zone defense which will result in good scoring opportunities. As the ball is passed from No. 3 to No. 2 to No. 1, the movements of the players

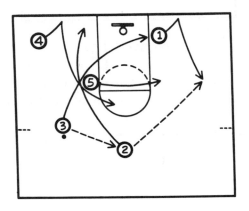

DIAGRAM 7-26

would be as shown in the diagram. The first cutter would be No. 3 and he would fill the *number 4* position on the opposite side. No. 5 stays in the *number 5* position while No. 4 comes out to the *number 2* position. No. 2 moves down to the *number 1* position on the weak side and No. 1 fills the *number 3* position. The possibilities of the ball being passed from No. 1 to No. 3, 5, 4, or from these players to other players, are great indeed.

To play against a zone the offense must accomplish the following:

1. Find the weak spots in the defense.
2. Drive when possible.
3. Move the men—don't glue them to a spot on the floor—this offense provides movement.
4. Don't telegraph passes—use deception.
5. Find the point at which the defensive men break-off on following the offensive man in, and attack here.
6. Fast break when possible never allowing the defense to get set.

POINTS OF SPECIAL EMPHASIS FOR THE SHUFFLE

1. Timing is important in the Shuffle offense and the one play that needs perfect timing is the "change of sides."

2. The pass around the horn from the *number 3* position to No. 2 to No. 1 must be made quickly. If there is any delay on the pass from No. 2 to No. 1, the "change of sides" play will not be successful and should not be used.

3. No. 3 should always fake before passing to No. 2—this will help keep the defensive pressure off No. 2.

4. If the defensive man covering No. 3 is playing tight, No. 5 should move out more to close the gap making it possible to brush the defensive man off as No. 3 cuts by No. 5.

5. No. 5 should not be aggressive with setting the screen. The responsibility for the screen is on No. 3 who maneuvers his defensive man into the screen. No. 5 just holds his position.

6. The cut that the No. 3 player makes by the player in the No. 5 position on the "change of sides" maneuver should be to the right side (top side) about 90% of the time.

7. The player in the *number 1* position should play as close to the free throw lane as possible. This will make it possible for the pass from No. 2 to reach No. 1 in time for a short pass to No. 3 just after he cuts by No. 5. Before coming out for a pass, No. 1 should always fake to the baseline.

8. The timing of the cut by No. 3 on the "change of sides" is very important. He should start out slowly, then change pace in a burst of speed going by No. 5 just after No. 1 receives the ball.

9. If No. 3 is not open, he should move on out of the lane and No. 1 should get out of the hole immediately. This can be accomplished by doing the following: (a) shoot; (b) dribble out to the *number 3* position in a hurry; (c) do anything that could be done from the *number 3* position.

10. Whether the ball is dribbled or passed to the *number 2* position, the player in the *number 4* position *always goes to the baseline.* With this move, no matter what the offense does, he is in position to go to the key spots.

11. After No. 3 clears No. 5, No. 5 should feint back toward the basket and to his right and outside before coming back to the top of the circle and the *number 2* position.

12. The feeding pass from No. 1 to No. 3 should nearly always be a bounce pass under the hands and arms of the defensive player. This will keep No. 3 down low so that he will move to the basket under full control. The ideal spot to make this pass to him is about at the broken circle

area of the free throw lane, or from one and one-half to two strides after he has cleared the screen set by No. 5.

13. During the "change of sides" there should be no crowding of the middle since No. 3, 1, and 4 break to their new positions in this move. The first cut is by No. 3, then the movement by No. 1, followed by the cut to the new *number 5* position by No. 4.

14. When No. 3 starts a dribble toward No. 2 or No. 4, the player in the *number 5* position should station himself opposite the free throw line or higher to furnish an easier screening target.

15. In the "rolling game" the players should look for shots at all times.

16. The offensive players should know how the defense is playing at all times.

17. Don't hold the ball—keep it moving.

18. The focus of attention should be on the player in the *number 3* position. He is the quarterback.

19. Use the "change of sides" pattern as many times as is necessary in practice so that it can be executed perfectly under game conditions.

ADVANTAGES OF THE SHUFFLE OFFENSE

1. It works well against all defenses.
2. It gives opportunity for free lance play from a set pattern.
3. It does not have to have the big pivot-post player to make it successful.
4. The offense does not depend upon the pivot-post position for movement and action and the maneuvers can be executed with or without the ball being passed into this position.
5. It prevents the defense from using their men in certain positions unless they play a zone.
6. It is a true team offense and the players like it.
7. It establishes definite rebounding responsibilities.
8. It gives a well balanced attack with good out-shooting and good driving possibilities.
9. It provides good movement opportunities for all players.
10. Its flexibility makes it tough to scout.
11. Each player must learn more basketball by playing each position in the offense.
12. The offense is not complicated. It is easy to learn and bad passing and mistakes are reduced to the minimum because of this fact.

8

The Pick and
Roll Offense

There are basic principles to consider when selecting an offense and the coach should consider and weigh the advantages and disadvantages of each before deciding which one to use. These principles are: (1) The offense must fit the material or personnel available. (2) The offense should involve the basic fundamentals and ingredients of good sound basketball. The fundamentals which are taught should be those which fit into the general pattern of play. (3) The offense should require uniform floor balance so that uniformity can be accomplished. (4) All five men should be potential scorers and all five men should be moving so that the defense cannot slack off or sag on the better ball players. (5) The offense should have continuity of movement so that one maneuver will carry the player into another; yet there should be opportunity for individual and free-lance play. (6) The offense should force the defense to play over the entire court instead of confining its efforts to specific areas.

The trend in modern basketball has been away from the pattern style of play. There are those who believe that basketball has lost its elements of team play and that it has evolved into one-, two-, and three-man offensive maneuvers. The thinking behind this belief is that it is possible to isolate one man and let him operate on his own. The theory is that a good offensive player can beat a good defensive player. This situation has been brought about by rule changes permitting more leeway in the execution of the dribble, and the fade-away jump shot, which in turn makes it more difficult for the defensive player to guard the shooter and dribbler. This theory is without question basically sound and, while it is true that more and more teams are attempting to use such an offense, it is also true that a number of offenses employ many of the maneuvers which exist in the Pick and Roll offense without realizing it. Many coaches must rely on an offense pattern which will take advantage of certain types of players or average players. It is impossible for them to use the one- or two-man game because they do not have outstanding offensive players. This necessitates the employment of a system which will compensate for the inabilities of the personnel and which will create definite scoring situations. The Pick and Roll is such an offense. It is a moving offense and involves a great deal of picking or screening and ballhandling in order to shake a player loose for a good shot or a chance to drive to the basket.

The Pick and Roll offense is a direct outgrowth of the 3-out 2-in offense and was popularized about 1945 and used extensively by many outstanding and successful coaches since then. Many of the patterns used in the Pick and Roll bear close similarity to those maneuvers used in the 3-out 2-in offense.

The Pick and Roll offense depends upon the one-on-one or two-on-two principles which have dominated present-day basketball. It demands disciplined team play with all players being involved in sharing the offensive responsibilities.

Teamwork and team play are necessary in this offense; however, it is possible to utilize the individual abilities of each player. It is an imaginative offense and uses the creativeness of the players by allowing a certain amount of free-lance play. The players are not bound to a set pattern but the pattern serves as a basis for continuity of play. Each play has options which may be used as the circumstances arise. The use of these options is dictated by the players themselves and they must make these decisions dependent upon the extenuating circumstances present at the time of their anticipated use. However, it should be uppermost in the minds of all players that teamwork and team play are essential if the offense is successful. Therefore, the pattern must be followed if continuity of play is to be assured.

It should be remembered that teams using pattern offenses stress teamwork and team play by all team members. Good players help any offense to function successfully and the Pick and Roll offense is no exception.

THE PURPOSE OF THE PICK AND ROLL

The Pick and Roll offense is a deliberate, planned attack and is very effective against the man-to-man style of play. The offense provides for continuity of movement, teamwork, free-lance opportunities and good scoring possibilities.

The offensive position of the players and the offensive maneuvers result in spreading the defense. This permits an open style of play enabling the players to cut to the basket easily after a successful pick or screen. Scoring opportunities are not always the result of team play. The individual player's ability and creativeness can be utilized with success. Team play is fundamental and essential among all the personnel if the pattern is to be productive. While each potential play has options and variations that may be used depending on the circumstances involved, it is up to the individual players to make these decisions. Teamwork is essential to make the total effort successful.

Fundamentally the offense is designed to result in the close-in shot. This can be accomplished if the play is successful because the defense is spread, making it difficult for the defense to shift on the potential scorer. Keeping the offense well spread tends to spread the defense. Then with the defense well spread and with proper execution of the Pick and Roll, it is possible to work the ball in close for the layup. In order to do this, it is necessary to keep possession of the ball once it is obtained. It should be impressed on all the players that possession of the ball is all important. Don't lose it until a good shot at the basket is obtained. Set plays based on the Pick and Roll principles will assure the good shots.

However, it should be remembered that just because a team is using a set pattern of attack, it does not mean that the individual fundamentals should be neglected. No pattern is better than its execution and the players should be thoroughly drilled on those skills that go with the chosen type of play. Ballhandling, shooting, and passing cannot be over stressed. Good shooting wins games and most good scoring opportunities are the result of good passing and ballhandling.

The ultimate success of any offense depends upon whether it is the correct offense to use for the material available. The success of the players depends upon how well they are executing the skills necessary for the offense that is being used and how well they are operating within the chosen pattern of play.

PICK AND ROLL PERSONNEL

In order for the Pick and Roll offense to function effectively, it is necessary, as in any offense, to have players who can execute the skills required of such an offense. In order that the Pick and Roll offense may be used successfully, the three front or outside players should be clever passers, fakers, dribblers, smooth ballhandlers, threats with the long shot, and be able to score while driving in fast. These three front men do a great deal of picking and rolling. They are continually passing the ball back and forth, maneuvering for position, and watching for a chance to drive in for the layup.

The middle man is the trigger man in this offense and handles the ball a great deal of the time. He should spend considerable time with shooting from the outside since he will have occasion to do this quite frequently. He should be a player with a great deal of confidence and poise. He should be the quarterback, take-charge type of player who can size up the situation instantly and make the correct decision at precisely the right time.

The inside men should line up directly across from each other. They should be good strong rebounders and love contact, take great pride in beating opponents off the board and, in addition, possess good hook and turn shots. They should be able to take their place in the weave should the occasion demand it. They may exchange positions frequently by screening for one another, performing pick-and-roll situations, occasional hi-lo patterns and act as pivot men as the situation dictates.

The most important factor in the Pick and Roll offense is the movement of the players. Each player is encouraged to use his own initiative to create scoring opportunities. However he must not deviate from the pattern constantly; otherwise, the continuity of play will break down and the purpose of the pattern will be destroyed. The player's decision to break the pattern will be dependent upon his judgment as to whether he can beat his opponent or place his opponent at a disadvantage defensively. The better the personnel, the more freedom of action may be allowed. The Pick and Roll offensive maneuvers are so designed as to allow the good player to act on his own should the opportunity present itself. Some free-lance play is difficult to defend against and therefore should be encouraged. As the players become more experienced, they will become more adept in their judgment of when to use the free-lance maneuver.

Very seldom does a coach have what he would call perfect material; therefore, an offensive pattern must be used which will take advantage of the available material. A winning combination can be developed without the ideal material. However, any pattern style of play, including the Pick and Roll, demands a high degree of teamwork and cooperation. A selfish player has no place in this style of play because every effort of every player is being made to obtain the high-percentage shot.

The Pick and Roll offense demands that every player be able to play every position fairly well, since all five will have excellent opportunities to score using this pattern. All players should be able to drive well. The inside men being the strongest rebounders shoud be able to move into the position if the situation demands it. Both should be able to score from this position and also be able to move into the outside position if necessary.

ADVANTAGES OF THE PICK AND ROLL

1. Basic basketball fundamentals are used.
2. Good floor balance is maintained.
3. There is good movement of all offensive players.
4. There is continuity of play.
5. There is opportunity for free-lance play.
6. The defensive players are forced to play in many different areas of the court.
7. The big defensive men are taken away from the basket.
8. There is good distribution of scoring among all five players.
9. Good ballhandling is encouraged.
10. Good percentage shots are obtained.
11. The offense is equally effective from either side and center of the court.
12. The players are in specific areas at all times.
13. The one-on-one situation often prevails.
14. It is an aggressive, fast moving offense that carries the play to the opposition.
15. There is provision for uniformity of play.
16. There is provision for definite player assignments.
17. The offense can be broken down into separate drills.
18. The defensive players are forced to switch.
19. Teamwork and team play is encouraged and provided for.

DISADVANTAGES

1. The position of the offensive players results in poor rebound position.
2. All players must be excellent ballhandlers.
3. There must be perfect timing on all plays for successful completion.
4. All the players must exert extensive concentration in order to execute the plays.
5. All players must possess all around skills in the fundamentals.
6. The offense is fairly difficult to learn.
7. Excellent teamwork is necessary.
8. Ball possession is fundamental.
9. A certain kind of personnel is required.
10. Disciplined team play is necessary.

CONTINUITY OF PLAY

A good offense should have continuity of play. Every player should move to a designated or predetermined spot as the pattern unfolds and an option is completed. The Pick and Roll offense is designed for team scoring effort. It prevents the defense from concentrating on any one player as all players are potential scorers. The defense must concentrate on all players; consequently, there will be good team scoring effort. This situation results in good team morale and a willingness among the players to work together in an effort to help each other. Consequently, each player works harder in his effort because each knows that his opportunity to score will be forthcoming providing he carries out his assigned duties. This, of course, is the secret to team play. Although it may be possible to create the spirit of sacrifice for the good-of-the team idea, it is far more effective if each player knows that his sacrifice through the performance of his duties will not only aid his teammate in obtaining a shot but eventually will result in his own chances of scoring.

FLOOR BALANCE

Any type or style of pattern play demands proper floor balance. Although it is not necessary that players adhere to the pattern at all times, they must follow the prescribed pattern to such a degree that their teammates will know what movements are to be made and base their own movements on what is being done by their teammates. This does not mean that free-lance movements should not be attempted, but unless the players follow the prescribed pattern of play the continuity of play will be destroyed. Each player should be encouraged to use his own initiative as the situation demands, but only to the extent that he is able to take advantage of a lapse in the defense tactics of the opponents.

It is important in the Pick and Roll offense that the middle of the offensive area to be kept open so that the drive to the basket can be made after the pick. The players should be well spread out and not bunched in their respective positions. The Pick and Roll offense demands good ball-handling. Very few mistakes can be made in passing, receiving and dribbling. Both the ball and the personnel must be moved. It is a moving offense and no one can stand around. The more the ball and players move, the better as such movement will induce and cause defensive mistakes, which in turn will result in offensive success. The Pick and Roll offense makes the defense move and a defense that has to make a lot of moves makes a lot of mistakes which the offense can take advantage of.

The Pick and Roll offense always moves the ball toward the basket and into the scoring area. The proper spacing of the players will provide the players more room for maneuverability.

The fact that the two inside men break into the pivot position occasionally does not necessarily mean that the offense will result in a double pivot type of offense. This is done only in the event that it is difficult for the outside men to pass the ball to any other teammate. Any time the ball is passed into the post, there should be two men cutting in a scissors motion. Usually the passer will cut first and then will be followed by the other player in the best position which would be from the opposite side of the post. Any player cutting through the lane who does not receive the pass should clear the lane as quickly as possible. The players moving into the post position should always move to the ball.

SUMMARY

The Pick and Roll offense demands a well disciplined team and places great stress on team play. However, it does place emphasis on the one-on-one and two-on-two moves which are very much a part of present-day basketball. It encourages free lance play yet offers an opportunity for use of a pattern which produces scoring opportunities for every team member. It requires the defensive players to play in all areas of the court.

There are several principles or rules which must be adhered to if the Pick and Roll offense is to be successful. These are as follows:

1. The dribbler should attempt to take his opponent into the pick. He should not give him an opportunity to see if he is going to be picked. To do this the dribbler must drive hard making it difficult for his opponent to stay with him and watch for the pick at the same time.
2. The picker should not wait until the dribbler takes his opponent into the pick. He should advance to the dribbler. The pick should preferably take place near the high shooting percentage area if the dribbler is expected to shoot.
3. The dribbler should always keep an eye on the picker so that he can get the pass to him after the roll.
4. The dribbler should never stop his dribble until he is ready to shoot or pass off.
5. The roller should always use a reverse pivot and place himself between the basket and the man he has picked. He should also keep an eye on the ball.

6. The lob pass is the best pass to use and it should be short so that it will not be intercepted.

Diagram 8-1 shows the original or starting position of the players in the Pick and Roll offense. The outcourt players No. 1, 2 and 3 are spaced evenly apart, are well spread and in a straight line. The inside players No. 4 and No. 5 are lined up slightly to the inside of No. 1 and No. 3, as shown in the diagram. No. 4 and No. 5 may also assume the pivot position at any time or break to the outside in order to receive a pass should the outcourt players find themselves unable to begin the regular pattern of play. No. 1 and No. 3 may also move up a yard toward the basket if the Pick and Roll plays are to be used or the defense is sagging thereby making it difficult for the players to cut.

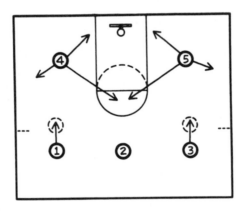

DIAGRAM 8-1

Diagram 8-2 shows No. 2 passing to No. 1 and then following the pass and setting a pick for No. 1. No. 2 breaks toward No. 1 immediately after making the pass and sets the pick as soon as possible. No. 1 fakes to his left and then dribbles off the pick that has been set for him by No. 2. After No. 1 makes his drive, No. 2 moves away from his screening position and takes the position formally occupied by No. 1. No. 1 drives toward the basket and goes all the way in for the layup, if it is possible to do so. If No. 1 cannot go all the way for the layup, he pivots and passes off to No. 3 who, as soon as he has seen No. 1 make his drive, has faked to his right

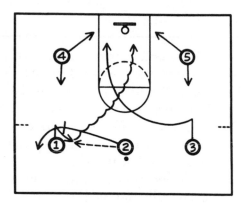

DIAGRAM 8-2

and cut behind No. 1. The player guarding No. 1 has a great deal of pressure put upon him because, if he does not switch, No. 1 may be able to drive for the basket unmolested. If he does shift, No. 1 can execute a jump shot.

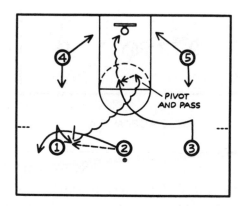

DIAGRAM 8-3

Diagram 8-3 shows a variation from the same play shown in Diagram 8-2. No. 2 passes to No. 1 who dribbles toward the basket. If No. 1 cannot drive all the way in for the layup, he stops, pivots and hands off to No. 3

who has faked to his right and driven behind No. 1. No. 4 and No. 5 should stay in their positions so that the middle of the free throw lane area is open. No. 3, after receiving the pass-off from No. 1, drives in for the layup.

Diagram 8-4 shows the same pattern as in the previous two diagrams except that No. 3 drives behind No. 1 as No. 1 dribbles toward the basket. If No. 1's guard does not shift and No. 3's guard does not shift, No. 1 passes to No. 3 who will be free under the basket. No. 4 and No. 5 keep clear of the free throw lane area, but both drive to the board for a rebound as soon as it is evident that a shot is being attempted. In all three of the previous diagrams a jump shot from the high percentage area may be attempted should the opponents get screened out, fail to switch, or at any time the situation is favorable for such a shot.

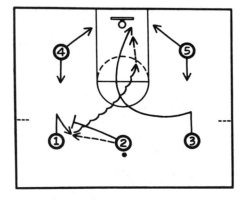

DIAGRAM 8-4

Diagram 8-5 shows No. 2 passing to No. 1 and picking for No. 1. No. 1 should fake in toward the basket in order to throw his guard off balance so as to be in a more favorable position to receive the pass. No. 2 and No. 3 may also exchange positions to make it easier to make the pass to No. 1. After the pick, No. 1 dribbles behind No. 2 and in toward the free throw lane area. No. 2 hesitates and then swings back into the position formerly occupied by No. 1. No. 3, upon seeing No. 1 driving to the free throw lane, fakes to his right and drives to his left behind No. 1 as No. 1

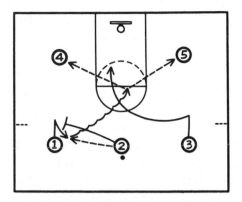

DIAGRAM 8-5

approaches the free throw area. If No. 1 cannot drive in all the way for the layup, he has the option of passing off to either No. 4 or No. 5, depending upon which of their guards shift off to cover him. No. 4 or No. 5 can either drive or shoot from their positions.

Diagram 8-6 shows No. 2 passing to No. 1 and then picking for No. 3. No. 3 and No. 2 exchange positions. No. 4, upon seeing the pass being made to No. 1, comes up from his position and picks off No. 1's guard from behind. No. 1 drives to his left and, as he does so, No. 4 rolls off the pick

DIAGRAM 8-6

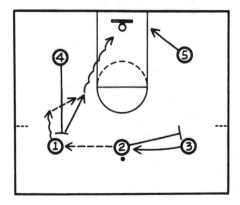

toward the basket. No. 1 may pass No. 4 the ball if he is open, which he will be if a switch on the part of the defensive player is made. If the switch is made, No. 1 keeps the ball and drives to the basket since No. 4 will have picked up No. 1's guard. No. 5 goes to the board for the rebound.

Diagram 8-7 shows the same maneuver on the opposite side of the floor. No. 2 passes the ball to No. 3 and goes to the opposite side of the floor and picks for No. 1. No. 3 starts a driving dribble down the right side of the floor. No. 5, upon seeing No. 3 starting his dribble, comes up behind No. 3's guard and picks. No. 3 continues the dribble and, if No. 5's guard makes a switch on No. 3, No. 5 executes a roll and drives to the basket. With this maneuver, if executed correctly, No. 5 will be open for a pass and a clear path to the basket for a layup. This maneuver between No. 3 and No. 5 should be timed correctly so that the pick and roll will free either No. 5 or No. 3. No. 4 will go to the basket for the rebound.

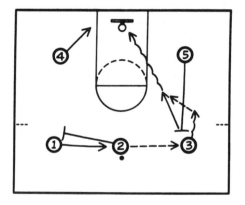

DIAGRAM 8-7

Diagram 8-8 shows No. 1 passing to No. 2. No. 1, No. 2 and No. 3 may maneuver until such time that the middle man is free to receive the pass. This player need not necessarily be player No. 2 but in this particular situation will be the middle man. After the pass to No. 2, No. 1 will move forward and pick for No. 2, who immediately dribbles to his left. After No. 2 has begun his dribble, No. 1 rolls from his pick using a reverse pivot and drives for the basket. If the pick is executed correctly,

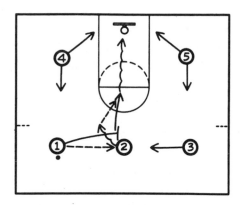

DIAGRAM 8-8

No. 1 will be free for the pass down the middle from No. 2. This pass should be in the form of a lob pass. No. 4 and No. 5 should move out from the free throw area until such time as they are needed for rebound purposes.

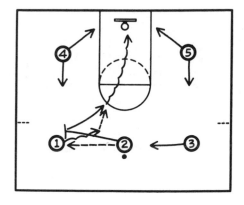

DIAGRAM 8-9

Diagram 8-9 shows the Pick and Roll from the left side of the floor. No. 2 passes to No. 1. After the pass No. 2 follows thru and picks for No. 1. No. 1 dribbles to his right and, at the same time, No. 2 executes a reverse pivot and drives toward the basket. No. 1 passes to No. 2 using a lob pass. If the players guarding No. 1 and 2 do not shift, then No. 1 will continue to dribble and drive all the way down the middle for the layup. If the guards do switch and No. 2 executes the pick and roll correctly, No. 2 will be open for a lob pass from No. 1 and a clear path to the basket. This is the two man offensive maneuver which is so prevalent in present day basketball.

Diagram 8-10 shows the Pick and Roll from the center of the court and originating from the right side of the floor. No. 3 passes the ball to No. 2 in the center of the court. Should it be difficult for this pass to be made No. 1, 2 and 3 should execute a weave out in the front court until such time as it is possible to make the pass and execute the Pick and Roll. It will also be easier to make the correct pass if the guards are playing No. 1, 2 and 3 loosely. No. 3 follows the pass made to No. 2 and sets a pick. No. 2 dribbles the ball across the court. As soon as this dribble is started, No. 3 executes the roll-off by doing a reverse pivot, placing No. 2's guard to his back. No. 3 then drives to the basket straight down the center of the free throw lane. No. 2 makes a lob pass to No. 3 as he breaks down the lane for the layup.

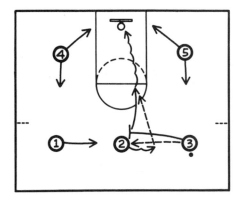

DIAGRAM 8-10

Diagram 8-11 shows No. 2 passing to No. 3. No. 2 follows the pass and picks for No. 3. No. 3 fakes to his right and, if able to do so, dribbles

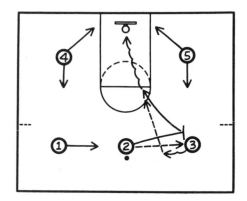

DIAGRAM 8-11

to his left until such time as No. 2, after he has made his pick, rolls toward
the basket. No. 3 passes the ball, using a lob pass, to No. 2 near the free
throw line area. If No. 3's and No. 2's guards switch, it will leave No. 2
open as No. 2's guard will switch to No. 3. If there is no switching of
guards, then No. 3 will be free to drive around No. 2 and straight into
the free throw lane area. All these front line plays are designed for the
two men working together in a Pick and Roll situation. No. 4 and No. 5
will keep the free throw lane area open so that the player may drive
thru for the layup and it will be easier to make the lob pass on the roll
off after the pick. Both No. 4 and No. 5 will go to the boards after they
see the player free for the shot.

It is important at this time to mention that the following diagrams
indicate that the three outcourt men are involved in most of the plays.

Diagram 8-12 shows how the inside men may be brought into the
pattern and provide it with the necessary continuity of play so important
in modern day pattern basketball. If No. 2, after executing a screen for
No. 3, wants to go into the continuity pattern, he continues to the corner
and screens for No. 5. No. 5 moves to the outside and follows the passing
and screening pattern looking for the drive-in each time he handles the
ball. The opposite side forward No. 4 may be brought into the continuity
in the same manner. Another way in which No. 4 and 5 may be brought
into the continuity is to have them break to a post position. The outside
players are then able to pass to the post man and scissor off him.

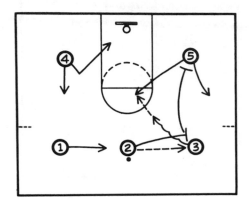

DIAGRAM 8-12

Diagram 8-13 shows a continuation or variation of the play shown in Diagram 8-11 if No. 1 is able to drive to the free throw line area but no further. Instead of breaking out to meet No. 1, No. 5 remains stationary. No. 1 passes to No. 5 and continues on to set a pick for No. 5. No. 5 attempts to dribble and drive to the basket. If he cannot do this, he passes to No. 4 who has been freed by a pick from No. 3. No. 1 also rolls to the

DIAGRAM 8-13

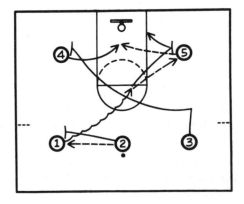

basket after picking for No. 5 and he also may receive the pass from No. 5. No. 3 fakes to his right and waits until No. 1 has made his drive before he picks for No. 4.

Diagram 8-14 shows the Pick and Roll being executed for the deep man. The middle man No. 2 makes the pass to No. 3 who in turn dribbles toward the center of the floor and to the outside of No. 2 who has set a pick for him. As soon as No. 1 sees that No. 3 has started his dribble, he drives down the left side of the floor and sets a pick for No. 4. No. 4 cuts around No. 1 and receives a pass from No. 3. If No. 4 does not break across to the free throw area after receiving a pick from No. 1, then No. 1 makes a reverse pivot and rolls to the basket. No. 1 then receives the pass from No. 3.

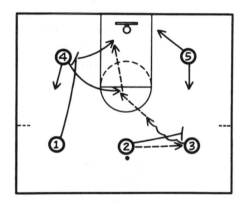

DIAGRAM 8-14

Diagram 8-15 shows the same kind of beginning maneuver as in Diagram 8-14. No. 2 passes the ball to No. 3 and then moves over and picks for No. 3. No. 3 fakes or dribbles to free himself and passes to No. 4 who has moved into the high post pivot position. No. 2 holds the pick momentarily and then pivots, rolls and drives past No. 4 to his left. No. 1, seeing No. 2 making his drive, cuts directly behind No. 2 thereby brushing off his guard. No. 2 and No. 1 cut in a scissors movement and No. 4 will pass to either of the players as they make their cuts. No. 3 holds his position outcourt.

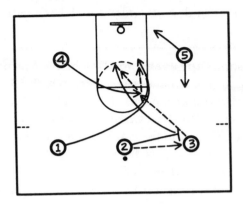

DIAGRAM 8-15

Diagram 8-16 shows players No. 1, 2 and 3 executing a three-man weave out front in order to free a player for a pass into the pivot. This brings the corner man into the pattern. Timing is important, for No. 5 must break out to meet the pass, but at the same time avoid interfering with the players who might as a result of a proper pick be driving through. If No. 5 decides to break into the pivot position, he should do so with the idea that he will receive the pass. If the outcourt players don't free a player for a drive-in or good set shot by using the three man weave they

DIAGRAM 8-16

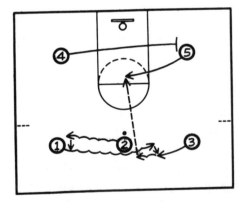

can use either No. 5 or No. 4 as post men to scissors off of. The post man should maneuver for all passes made to him, moving toward the ball.

Diagram 8-17 shows the Pick and Roll using the corner man No. 5. The diagram shows No. 3 passing the ball to No. 5 although, as has been mentioned, No. 1, 2 and 3 should maneuver in such a manner so that it is possible for the outside player (which in this particular case is No. 3) can make the pass to No. 5. No. 3 will follow the pass to No. 5 and set a pick to the inside for him. No. 5 will dribble to the outside of the pick, around No. 3, and attempt a drive to the basket. Should No. 5 not be able to complete the drive, he immediately passes off to No. 3 who, after he has executed the pick, reverses pivots and rolls toward the basket. No. 2, or the player in the middle position, drives across court and picks for No. 4 who drives around No. 2 and toward the basket where he receives a pass from No. 5, if No. 5 is not able or cannot make the pass to No. 3.

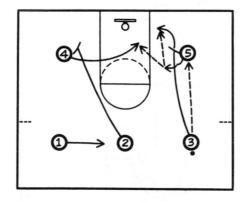

DIAGRAM 8-17

Diagram 8-18 shows No. 2 passing to No. 3. No. 2 follows the path of the ball and receives a return pass from No. 3 on the outside using No. 3 as a shield. No. 2 tries to dribble down the court, but if he cannot do so he passes to No. 5 who comes out to meet the ball. No. 2 continues his drive toward No. 5 and sets a pick on the inside for No. 5. No. 5 dribbles off the pick and drives to the basket. If he cannot do this because No. 2's man shifts, then No. 2 rolls and receives a pass from No. 5. No. 1,

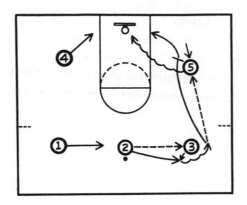

DIAGRAM 8-18

2 and 3 should maneuver so that No. 2 or the player on the outside is able to make the pass to No. 5. No. 5 will need to make the decision as to whether he is able to dribble in for the layup or pass off to No. 2 who has rolled toward the basket after the pick. No. 4 will go to the board as soon as he sees either No. 2 or No. 5 go in for the shot or shoot from the outside. No. 1 holds a position out front.

DIAGRAM 8-19

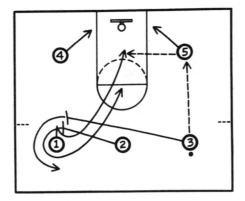

Diagram 8-19 shows No. 3 passing to the corner man No. 5. No. 5 fakes in toward the basket and then out to meet the ball. After the pass is made, No. 2 and No. 3 set a double pick for No. 1. No. 1 fakes to his left, delays, and then cuts off the double pick as shown in the diagram. No. 2 holds the pick until No. 1 has made his cut, then he executes a reverse pivot and rolls off the pick toward the basket. He receives the pass from No. 5 as he nears the free throw area depending upon where he is free to receive the pass. No. 3 takes his position in the area vacated by No. 1 and No. 2 to protect against an intercepted pass. No. 4 drives to the board for the rebound or moves out to the outside area if needed.

Diagram 8-20 shows players No. 1 and No. 3 moved up slightly and players No. 4 and 5 stationed deeper and closer to the free throw lane area. This play is a simple give-and-go type play. If No. 2 is able to get a half step on his opponent, he receives a pass from No. 1 and goes for the layup. If No. 2 does not receive the pass from No. 1, he moves across and screens for No. 4. No. 4 will cut off the screen provided by No. 2 or move out and take the place of No. 1 depending upon the effectiveness of the pick. If No. 4 cannot drive in for the layup, he stations himself in the post position. No. 2 returns to the outside position.

DIAGRAM 8-20

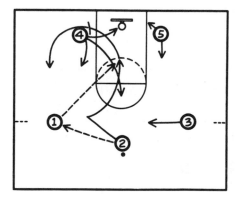

Diagram 8-21 shows the ball being passed from No. 2 to No. 1 and the screen being made to the opposite side to which the pass is made. This play works exceedingly well if the opposition is sagging and the screen can be made deep enough to allow No. 3 to fake his opponent to the outside and then run him into the screener No. 2. If No. 3 is not able to free himself to such an extent that he is unable to either execute a jump shot or drive in for a layup, he stops, pivots and passes off to the cutters No. 1 and No. 2. If No. 1 or No. 2 don't receive the pass, they should screen for Nos. 4 and 5.

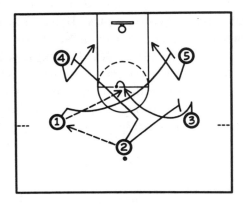

DIAGRAM 8-21

DIAGRAM 8-22

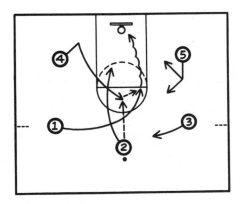

Diagram 8-22 shows No. 4 breaking into the high post and receiving a pass from No. 2. This maneuver can be executed at any time but works extremely well if the outcourt men are being pressed so closely that it is difficult to maneuver. No. 4 should time his cut to the post position at a time when No. 2 is ready to pass him the ball. No. 3 moves to the position formally occupied by No. 2 and No. 5 moves to the free throw area.

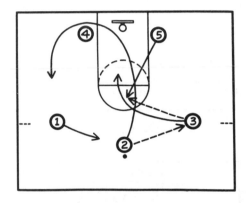

DIAGRAM 8-23

Diagram 8-23 shows players No. 4 and No. 5 playing tight to the free throw lane and close to the basket. This gives maximum rebounding strength and these players should be the best rebounders. Player No. 2 passes to No. 3 and cuts directly down the center of the free throw lane and goes to the opposite side of the floor. No. 1 takes the place formally occupied by No. 2. No. 2, after making his cut, takes the place of No. 1. No. 5 breaks into the pivot. The ball is passed to No. 5 in the pivot, and players scissor off of him.

Diagram 8-24 shows No. 1 passing to No. 2. After the pass is made by No. 1, he cuts to the weak side and deep under the basket. No. 3 takes the place of No. 2. No. 4 breaks into the pivot and No. 2 can either pass to No. 4 in the pivot and cut off of the pivot, or he can jump shoot from

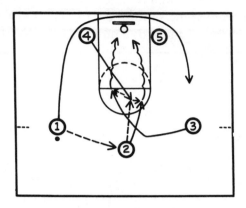

DIAGRAM 8-24

a return pass from No. 4. No. 1 cuts under the basket and returns to the outside position taking the position formerly occupied by No. 3.

DIAGRAM 8-25

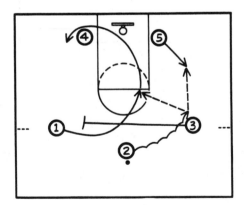

Diagram 8-25 shows No. 2 dribbling to the outside of No. 3. No. 3 screens for No. 1. No. 1 cuts behind the screen afforded him by No. 3. No. 2 can pass to No. 1 as No. 1 cuts toward the basket, execute a jump shot, or pass to No. 5.

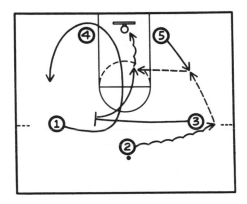

DIAGRAM 8-26

Diagram 8-26 shows a sequence to the previous play. No. 2 dribbles to the outside of No. 3 using him as a screen. No. 3 moves over to the top of the free throw circle where he screens for No. 1 who has moved over to meet him in that area. No. 1 cuts around No. 3 and moves down the free throw lane and out to his left returning to the outside position and taking No. 2's place. No. 3, after screening for No. 1, does a reverse pivot and drives down the free throw lane for the basket. Meanwhile, No. 2 has passed the ball to No. 5 who has broken out to the side and toward No. 2 to receive the pass. No. 5 passes to No. 3 as No. 3 drives toward the basket.

Diagram 8-27 shows the inside screen, with No. 2 dribbling and handing off to No. 3 who cuts to the outside. No. 3 continues the dribble in the opposite direction and hands off to No. 1 who is coming to meet him. No. 1 goes to the outside of No. 3 and takes the pass from No. 3. No. 1 continues the dribble and drives down the right side of the court

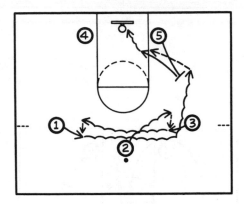

DIAGRAM 8-27

as shown in the diagram. No. 5 comes up from the tight position and sets a screen for No. 1 who can continue his drive to the basket or use a jump shot. No. 5 may roll after the screen and receive a pass from No. 1.

9

The Fast Break

The fast break, which revolutionized the game of basketball, first made its appearance in the early 1930's. Since then there have been many versions of the fast break, until at the present time it is used to some extent by almost every team playing the game.

Many coaches rely on the fast break entirely, others the slow break with a pattern offense, and still others with a combination of the two.

The fast break is the most potent weapon in basketball if it is carried out effectively. If not, it can lead to dire consequences. A good fast break cannot be taught "overnight"—it takes constant practice and dedicated players who are willing to condition themselves to the stamina needed to execute the fast-break patterns for an entire game. To be effective the fast break also takes players who are capable of performing the skills which are needed for the fast break patterns.

POPULARITY OF THE FAST BREAK

The fast break has proven to be very popular for various reasons, the most obvious being that of spectator appeal. There is no play in basketball that is as thrilling to the spectator, or satisfying to the player, as a basket resulting from a well executed fast break. This can happen time after time to the fast break team, if a well organized and planned attack stressing ball control is present. Mastery comes with hard work and practice so that with constant repetition the skills become part of the player's movements and he does them automatically.

The fast break must be sold to the players. They need to believe in it the same as any other offense. Usually this is not a difficult task since most players like this style of play. It is an offense, however, that demands certain player qualifications and abilities. Each player must possess agility, ballhandling ability, a certain amount of speed, and be in top physical condition if the fast break is to be successful.

PURPOSE OF THE FAST BREAK

The purpose of the fast break as we now think of it is not so much getting there first with the ball, as much as it is getting there with more offensive players than there are defensive players. This can be accomplished only with proper organization of personnel so that each player has a complete perspective of the entire situation and can do the job he is supposed to do at the correct time.

There are many ways to initiate the fast break. Probably the most popular is the three-lane fast break which will be discussed in this chapter. The fast break as described here does not stress the "solo" type basket obtained by the long pass over the entire defense. Rather, it stresses the controlled break that results in a situation whereby the offense outnumbers the defense long enough to take advantage of it and obtain a high-percentage shot.

Difference Between the Fast Break and Quick Break

The fast break is not to be confused with the *quick* break which is used only when possession of the ball is obtained at a time when the opposition is out of position defensively. The quick break can develop when the ball is stolen or a pass is intercepted, and the defensive players are caught out of position thereby enabling the team with the ball to break quickly down the floor for an easy layup.

The fast break team is usually one that is offensively minded and very often uses the quick break along with the press since the three tactics go well together. By using the press defensively and the fast and quick break offensively, it is possible to force the opponents into errors that they ordinarily would not make. The quick break team usually capitalizes on these errors and turns them into easy baskets. A running team is an aggressive team. It has the ability to get the quick basket thereby putting constant pressure on the defense.

USE OF THE PRESS WITH THE FAST BREAK

The press will prevent the opponents from slowing down the pace of the game—which, to a fast breaking team, is not desirable since most of the scoring opportunities will be the result of the fast style of play. The press will keep pressure on the offense, disrupt their pattern of play, upset their timing and generally harass them to the point where they will make mistakes and provide opportunities for the fast break and quick break to develop. Constant pressure on an offensive team will tend to destroy the poise of the opponents.

If a team loses its poise for just a short time, a pressing, fast breaking team can break a game wide open by a flurry of quick baskets and put the game out of reach. A pressing team will never allow the opposition to bring their offense to them. They will never allow the offense to "set up." They will harass them constantly, never allowing them to "run" their offense under ideal conditions.

IMPORTANCE OF ORGANIZATION

The fast break demands organization, and patterns need to be developed which will result in a definite continuity of play whereby each player knows exactly what to do under certain conditions. Every player must fit perfectly into this predetermined pattern of play and be able to adjust quickly to the changing conditions which present themselves with rapid regularity in the fast break style of play. In teaching these patterns, basic practice drills should be used which correspond to the patterns used in the fast break. If any style or type of offense is to be fully understood, it must be broken down into separate parts or drills. Each part can be used as a separate drill to be practiced daily until it becomes a habit. Each drill can then be fitted into the pattern of play. In this way every player will become accustomed to each position and fit himself into the pattern of play no matter where he finds himself after his team gains possession of the ball.

To simplify the fast break for the players, practically the same pattern should be used at all times. The guards and forwards have identical duties and will need to be able to perform efficiently in all three lanes. Each will need to become proficient in filling the lane nearest to him at the correct moment and carrying out the required duties of the player who should be in that particular lane. The patterns shown may be used from either a man-to-man style of defense or a zone. The assignments are practically the same. The center, usually being the biggest and best rebounder, does not help bring the ball down the floor and is used as a trailer. This also conserves his energy and lets him concentrate on defensive rebounding.

Players must be taught early that no team has a fast break offense unless it uses the three lanes for the fast break. The success of the fast break depends upon the skill of the players in handling, dribbling, and passing the ball while moving at top speed so that they can outmaneuver the defense. The fast break offense should never be forced. Certain principles should be adhered to. For instance, every effort should be made to fill the three lanes at all times. The two players in the outside lanes stay wide until they approach the basket. They then cut in toward the basket, and if the pass-off is not made to one of them, they cut underneath the basket. The outside men can be either the guards or the forwards. The trailer is usually the center. If the fast break is stopped, the middle man usually has the ball in the vicinity of the free-throw lane, where he stops until he is able to shoot or pass off to one of the side men.

A team need not be fast to be a good fast break team. It is the ability of the players to judge when ball possession is going to be obtained that determines the success of the fast break. The players should have the ability to start their movement down the floor in a systematic and organized fashion as soon as possible after they realize they have gained, or are about to gain, possession of the ball.

Transition from Defense to Offense

One of the big problems in the use of the fast break is the switching from the defense to offense. It is important that this changeover be made swiftly and that it fit into the regular pattern without a complete rearrangement of the personnel.

There are definite rules which should govern the fast break.

1. The guard should clear the ball to the corner of the court.
2. The ball should be taken down the side of the court to the center line to avoid mid-court congestion.
3. The pass should be made to the player in the center lane as he approaches the center of the court. He keeps the ball until such time as the defense commits itself. He stops at the free throw line.
4. All players should stay in their lanes and keep well spread out.
5. The center is the trailer. He should do the biggest share of the rebounding both offensively and defensively. As a trailer, he is able to conserve his energy.
6. The middle man should dribble the ball from the center circle where he receives it to the free throw line. He should not pass to the flankers unless it is necessary.

Fast-Break Opportunities

There are many theories involving the use of the fast break. A team may fast break from:

1. A rebounded missed shot
2. A rebounded missed free throw
3. A scoring situation by the opponents
4. A pass interception
5. An out-of-bounds situation
6. A loose-ball situation
7. A jump-ball situation

A good fast break team should have at least one set formation for each of the preceding situations. Remember that the primary purpose is to get three men against two, two men against one, or one man against none.

Keys to a Successful Fast Break

1. Make as few passes as possible
2. Refrain from taking poor shots
3. Lead the receiver
4. Have a predetermined pattern of attack
5. Practice constantly
6. Keep spread out
7. Give up the break if the offense is outnumbered
8. The outside men should be ahead of the middle man who has the ball.
9. The middle man should be prepared to hold up the play when necessary.
10. Don't cross-court pass. Keep the ball in the middle.
11. Keep the ball on the side of the court until it is possible to pass to the middleman at center court.
12. Don't let the fast break become fire-wagon basketball. Remember it is a controlled fast break.
13. Don't always work for the layup. A good outcourt shot is acceptable and occasionally even desirable if rebound strength is in evidence.
14. Talk it up. Let teammates know where you are and what you are doing.
15. Don't force the fast break.
16. Always move forward.
17. Free lance when the occasion demands.
18. Use trailers when needed.

Parts of the Fast Break

There are three parts to the fast break:

1. The defensive rebound and pass-out.
2. The break down the floor to outnumber the defense.
3. The scoring situation or the decision either to shoot or to pass.

Each of these situations must be fully understood and practiced by all of the players. It takes a great deal of practice to teach all five players to handle all the assignments in the fast break.

The success of an attempted fast break is contingent upon the first pass when the defensive team gains possession of the ball. Unless the out-pass is performed immediately and accurately upon ball possession, the fast break becomes ineffective. In all cases where the fast-break opportunity exists, it is the "first out-pass" which clears the ball and starts it toward scoring territory that determines the success of the fast break. The speed and completion of the pass will help set up the play at the scoring end of the court.

After an opponent's shot, each player should retain his opponent by defensive screening and at the same time fight for the rebound as his position dictates. As soon as the rebound is won, the player in possession of the ball clears it to the side of the court—before he returns to the floor, if possible. A few players may be able to rebound and hook the ball out before touching the floor. If the player cannot do this, he may fake, jump, and whirl for the pass-out, or he may fake and dribble out. He should fake with arms, shoulders, and head to clear himself as he drives out from under the backboard. Usually the rebounder fakes after reaching the floor, takes one low dribble toward the end line to clear the under-basket scramble, and jumps high to hook-pass out to the side. This, of course, consumes valuable time.

Some coaches prefer spot passes to get the ball out. The rebounder comes down with the ball in the conventional manner, feints, takes a step into a clear area, leaps into the air, spots his receiver, and passes the ball. This is a baseball type of pass and very effective.

All other players must now assume their roles and responsibilities, which means they must move to the areas dictated by the situation. Each player is charged with assuming the correct position, thereby providing the rebounder with an opportunity for the outlet pass.

The outlet pass is designated to mean the first pass after the defensive team obtains the ball. This could result from any of the fast break opportunities listed earlier. It does not necessarily refer to the rebounded missed shot, although presumably this is where most of the fast break opportunities will originate. There are other opportunities and they should not be minimized in importance because a good fast break team will not only take advantage of all fast break opportunities but will try to create them.

Rebounding position is important, and it is not always possible to have guards, forwards, and center in excellent position. Let us assume that the opponents have taken a shot and the defensive team has gained possession. The two players nearest the basket have gone in close, along with the center, to fight for the rebound. The two players farthest out have not dropped back too far toward the defensive backboard after the opponent's shot, preferring to lose a little defensive strength in order to gain offensively. The out-men go in closely enough to handle any high rebounds but not closely enough to get caught in any scramble for the ball under the basket. The center covers the area immediately in front of the basket, with the two in-players flanking him on either side in a triangle which is used as a screening device.

Knowing when to fast break is also important. A player must know when a teammate has possession of the ball and is able to instigate the fast break. A fast break team is fast break conscious at all times. The players break for the basket as fast as possible with the expectation that a goal will be scored. As soon as ball possession is secured by a player, he looks down the court. He must size up the situation immediately. Does his team have an advantage? How many teammates are in position to utilize the fast break pattern?

The second part of the fast break is the attempt to get the ball down the floor into scoring position. After the ball is cleared from under the basket to the side, it is dribbled up the side of the court in a hard, fast-driving dribble until such time as it may be passed to the middle man. It should not be passed to him until he has reached the center circle area. The reason for taking the ball up the side of the court is that there is far less congestion on the side than in the middle and therefore less chance for interception. The ball may be advanced faster for the same reason, and speed is essential in the fast break. The middle man keeps the ball all the way to the free throw line unless he is closely guarded or has a chance for a pass to a free man for a layup. Usually the opposition will not try to defend against the player who is advancing the ball up the sideline. It is too busy back-pedaling and covering the middle. The dribbler is thus able to move the ball quickly up to a position where it can be passed into the middle lane. The pass should be a two-handed pass for accuracy and speed. This pass is of extreme importance.

The third or scoring part of the offense has the middle man receiving the ball at the center circle and dribbling at top speed to the back of the free throw circle, then quickly slowing down to a controlled dribble to make one of the guards commit himself. At a time when one of the guards commits himself to the dribbler, the wing man is open to drive in for the layup. Usually the guards will give way until reaching their defensive free throw line. This is the area where the fast break is broken up and fails to materialize. The guard must have control of his body movements here because he must make the quick pass when his guard commits himself. Also, if the dribbler slows down as he crosses the free throw circle he can continue to the basket. If he sees an opening he can whip a quick pass off the dribble, or he can stop and take an easy shot from the free throw area. The dribbler also may drive to the free throw line, leave his feet in jump-shot fashion, fake a shot or a pass, and flip a quick pass as he leaves his feet. If the dribbler, after receiving the ball at the center circle, is challenged by a defensive player thus making it impossible for him to continue his dribble, he should feed the ball back to the sideline man. Good ballhandling is the backbone of the fast break.

The coach should insist that the fast break be controlled. A team using the fast break must be conscious of its uses at every possible opportunity. The fast break may be used even though a player does not shoot at the basket the moment he reaches scoring territory. A misconception many players have of the fast break is that it must finish with a shot at the basket at the earliest opportunity. It is much more profitable to retain possession of the ball if the odds are not in favor of taking a shot.

The success of the fast break at the scoring end depends upon the hesitation of the middle man at the free throw area. He must make the defensive men commit themselves. At this point the middle man has three options: (1) If one of the guards uses a fake and then drops back, the middle man may fake a pass and then shoot. (2) If one defensive man comes forward to challenge the middle man, he should make the pass off to the wing man on that side. (3) If both defensive men rush the middle man, he has a choice of passing to either side. He must stop at the free throw circle to make the guards commit themselves. Even with two on one, the middle man should dribble down and wait near the free throw circle for the defensive men to commit themselves, then shoot or pass off, whichever is better. This point is extremely important, since most players have a tendency to get rid of the ball while still in motion. By stopping, the dribbler is in an excellent position to pass off or, if the defense drops off to cover the side men, to take his time and shoot from within a high-percentage area.

Players should be allowed to shoot with relative freedom on the break, providing there are equal numbers or better down floor. The 12 to 16 foot jumper is a good percentage shot off the break, providing the shooter is free and able to get off a good shot without being pressured. He should refrain from taking a shot under pressure. This, of course, is difficult to coach.

The number one problem in executing the fast break is being over-anxious. Instead of making the defensive man commit himself, the player will either shoot too quickly or pass to a teammate who is covered. In developing a fast break attack, the player should remember that when the scoring zone is reached, the ball should be in possession of the player in the center of the court at the foul line.

CONCLUSION

In conclusion, it must be remembered that in the controlled fast break, the opponents will not always allow the offensive team to do the things it wants to do. The offense, therefore, should be elastic enough to allow for individual initiative to permit each player to capitalize on the particular situation as it exists. The illustrations shown will not include every fast break possibility but rather will present those which occur most frequently. The reader may improvise from the illustrations shown, as the pattern for all possibilities is similar once ball possession is secured.

It must be remembered that there are many ingredients that make up a successful fast break. First of all, there must be an aggressive defense which usually accompanies all fast break teams. The defense must force the offense into mistakes and be ready to capitalize on these mistakes at every opportunity. The moment a mistake is made the transition from defense to offense should be made. This should be done swiftly, smoothly, and automatically without any effort whatsoever. The regular pattern should unfold immediately and the players should assume their positions without hesitation. This comes through constant practice and with the use of drills which are a part of the pattern. The player's ability to judge when the fastbreak opportunity exists is all important.

Another ingredient is quick rebounding. This above everything else is the key to the success of the fast break. The rebounder must get the ball and make the outlet pass quickly. Delay here will slow down the fast break's chances of being successful. The pass must be released quickly and accurately.

The third ingredient is organization. Predetermined plans must be made and adhered to. Every player has a specific task to perform and he must be alert and ready to react to situations immediately and with purpose. He must know what to do at the correct time and under all conditions. He must be organized in his thoughts as well as in his actions.

The fourth ingredient is good judgment. Every player must know when to pass, when to dribble, and when to shoot. He should use good judgment in filling the lanes which is necessary if the fast break is successful.

The fifth ingredient is speed. The fast break does not place a premium on speed although it is desirable. The player who has a good change of pace and is a quick starter is more valuable in the fast break than the player who possesses great speed. Being able to judge the speed of a teammate will do much to determine the success of the pass.

The sixth ingredient is ballhandling. The team that cannot handle the ball should not fast break.

There are many other ingredients that are necessary to make up a successful fast break offense. It is the duty of the coach to determine if his players possess the needed talent to install this type of offense. No one can deny that it isn't a thrilling offense to coach, to watch, and to play.

Diagram 9-1 shows the basketball court divided into the different areas from where the specific skills are executed which make up the fast

DIAGRAM 9-1

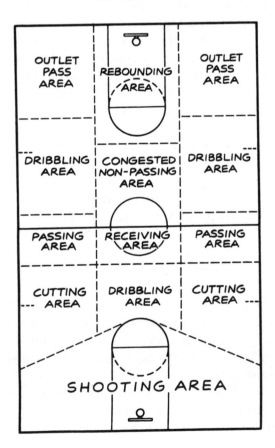

break pattern described in this chapter. There will naturally be variations and the skills will not always be executed in the areas indicated. However it can be assumed that this will usually be the case, keeping in mind that certain circumstances will alter the pattern and influence the conditions under which the skills are performed or executed. The rebounding area is shown to be an area where most of the rebounding from missed shots or missed free throws will occur. As has been stated previously fast break opportunities can arise from almost any position on the court and do not always need to begin from a rebounded missed shot or free throw. The areas shown in the diagram determine the rules which govern the fast break described in this chapter namely: (1) The rebounder should clear the ball to the corner of the court. (2) The ball should be taken down the side of the court in the non-congested area where it can be moved quickly and where mid-court congestion can be avoided. (3) The pass should be made to the player in the center lane as he approaches the center of the court. (4) The center player keeps the ball until such time as the defense commits itself. (5) The middle man should dribble the ball from the center circle where he receives it, to the free throw line. (6) All players should keep spread out and hold their positions.

The ball should be kept out of the congested area, which can be defined as the area from the top of free throw circle to the center circle, if at all possible. The chances of interception, fumble or tied up ball are by far the greatest in this area. A great deal of time will be wasted in getting the ball down court if it is moved into this congested area.

The ball can be advanced more rapidly even though it is by dribbling, by moving into the side court area where there is very little if any congestion. This gives the other players an opportunity to recover and move into the nearest lane to them.

By the time the ball is passed into the receiving area which is just beyond the center of the court the lanes are filled and a two-on-one or three-on-two situation has developed. The center player will be able to continue the dribble to the free throw area because the defensive players will try and protect the flanks, therefore it will not be too difficult to move the ball into scoring territory as indicated in the following diagrams.

Diagram 9-2 shows the rebound being made by No. 3 and the outpass to No. 1 at the side of the court. No. 5 usually is in front of the basket because he usually guards the pivot man. The two guards No. 3 and No. 4 should try and form a "V" around the basket area in an attempt to screen out the opposition. As the shot is taken all players should follow the flight of the ball and try and anticipate the spot where the ball will come off the board or basket. The defensive player should execute a

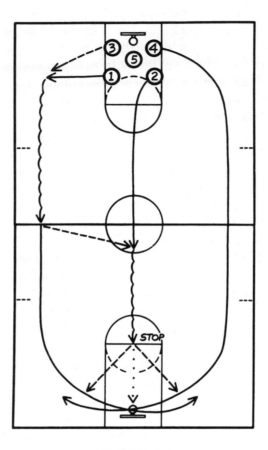

DIAGRAM 9-2

reverse pivot in the direction in which his opponent goes in his attempt to get the rebound. He should screen his opponent by placing his back to him, which will be done as a result of the reverse pivot, which will leave him facing the basket.

No. 1 and No. 2 should not attempt to drop back too far towards the defensive backboard but try and drop back far enough so that they are able to grab any rebounds that carom out that far. This will leave them in good position for the fast break when possession of the ball is obtained. As soon as No. 3 gains possession of the ball, No. 1 moves over to the side of the court as indicated in the diagram and receives the pass out from No. 3. No. 1 then dribbles down the side of the court until he is able to pass into No. 2 who has cut up the center of the court or center lane. No. 1 cuts up the outside lane and No. 4 cuts up the opposite outside lane thereby filling all three lanes. No. 2 always stops his dribble near the free throw circle area so that the guard must come out to take him thereby enabling No. 1 or No. 4 to be open for the pass and shot.

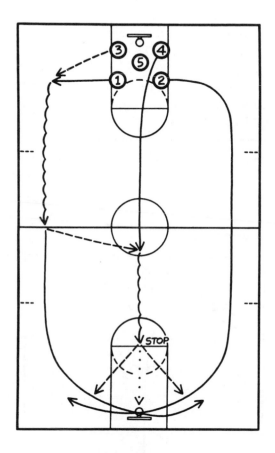

DIAGRAM 9-3

Diagram 9-3 shows the rebound made by No. 3 on a fast break play from a missed shot, or the same kind of situation as in the previous diagram. The setup is the same with No. 3 rebounding and making the outlet pass to No. 1 who has gone to the side of the court and established himself in the outside lane as soon as he is sure No. 3 has possession of the ball. No. 3 may get the ball to him by the quickest way possible which might entail a one handed jump pass, or he may be delayed and need to dribble free before he can make the pass. If No. 4 is in position in front of the basket as indicated in the diagram he immediately makes his move directly upcourt in the center lane after he has made sure that No. 3 has the ball and is ready to make the outlet pass to No. 1. No. 2 in the meantime moves into the other outside lane, thereby filling the three lanes. No. 1 brings the ball up the outside lane in a hard driving dribble until he is past or near the center line at which time he passes in to No. 4 who continues down the center lane using the dribble to a point near the free throw circle or free throw lane where he has several options. No. 4 may shoot from this area, he may drive in for the layup if the situation warrants it or he may pass off to No. 1 or to No. 2 who has filled the other outside lane. No. 1 or No. 2 may either shoot from outcourt or drive in for the layup dependant upon their judgment as to what should be done under the existing circumstances.

Diagram 9-4 shows another variation of the fast break from a missed shot. No. 3, 4 and 5 form the "V" in front of the basket with No. 1 and 2 further out toward the free throw line area. The placement of these

DIAGRAM 9-4

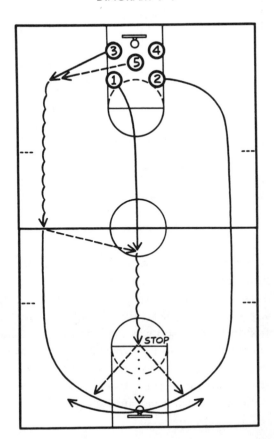

players will naturally depend upon where they are located at the time the shot is taken in relation to where the players they are guarding are at the time of the shot. However, as soon as the shot is taken, the three players nearest the board (who in this instance will be numbered No. 3 and 4) will attempt to station themselves in the position shown in the diagram. No. 1 and 2 should attempt to be in the immediate vicinity so that they can help with the rebounding if necessary. In this diagram No. 5 gets the rebound and passes to No. 3 who moves out to the side of the court and into the outside lane. No. 3 dribbles hard down the court and passes to No. 1, who has driven down the center lane expecting a pass from No. 3 after crossing the center of the court. No. 2 breaks down the other outside lane thereby filling all three lanes. No. 1 dribbles to the free throw area and executes one of the options as described in the previous diagrams.

It should be emphasized that the pass from the outside lane should not be made by No. 3 until he is at or beyond the center of the floor. No. 5 and No. 4 act as trailers and often are open should No. 1 be unable to pass to No. 3 and No. 2. Should No. 1 be unable to pass to No. 2 and No. 3 as they approach the basket, he may wait and see if they lose their guards as they cut under the basket.

Diagram 9-5 shows another variation of the fast break pattern from a missed shot. No. 3, 4 and 5 again attempt to form the "V" around the basket in an attempt to screen out the opposition. This must be done quickly so that the offensive players do not gain the inside rebounding position. Once this happens the value of the "V" is diminished considerably. The center No. 5 will usually be in the best rebounding position because his defensive position will usually be in the immediate vicinity of the basket due to the play of the offensive center. Here again, as the diagram shows, No. 5 will get the rebound and immediately make the outlet pass to No. 1. Usually the center is big enough to execute the outlet pass quickly. No. 1 moves out to the sideline as soon as he is sure that No. 5 has gained possession of the ball. After No. 1 receives the ball he dribbles hard down the side of the court and in the outside lane until he reaches the vicinity of center court, but still in the outside lane. No. 1, on approaching this position, looks for the player in the center lane (which in this situation is No. 2) who at the time the pass was made from No. 5 to No. 1 moved into the center lane and drove toward the offensive basket and toward the designated area where he was to receive the pass from No. 1. No. 4 meanwhile moved to the outside lane and upcourt as quickly

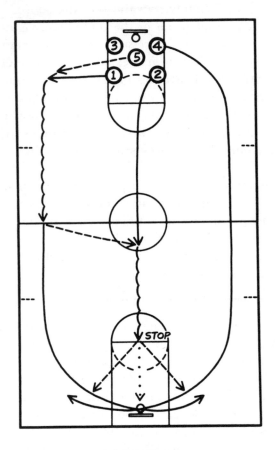

DIAGRAM 9-5

as possible after he realized that the out-pass had been made to No. 1 and the fast break was started. No. 1 and No. 4 should stay wide until such time as they make their cut toward the basket with the expectation of receiving a pass off from No. 2. Here again the pass from No. 1 should not be made until No. 2 has gotten beyond the center of the floor and the pass can be made in a less congested area thus assuring its success. As in the previous diagrams, No. 2 has the option of driving in, shooting from the free throw area, passing off to No. 1 or No. 4, or passing off to trailers No. 5 and No. 3.

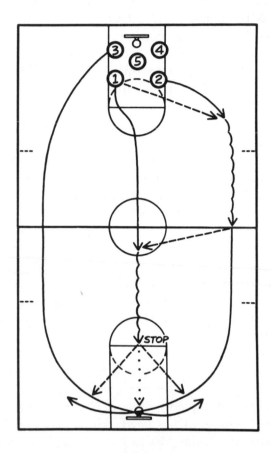

DIAGRAM 9-6

Diagram 9-6 shows another variation of the fast break from the missed shot, with the rebound coming off to No. 1 near the free throw area. No. 2 moves out to the outside lane either a little upcourt or directly to the side, depending upon whichever position is more conducive to receiving the pass from No. 1. No. 1 should be careful and use good judgment in making this pass since the chances of its being intercepted and turned into a quick basket by the opposition are enhanced in this situation because of the concentration of the players in this area. Therefore, it is possible that No. 1 will need to take a dribble or two downcourt or to the side so as to clear the ball for the pass and also enable No. 2 to gain time to get into proper position and make himself available for the pass from No. 1. As soon as No. 2 gains possession of the ball as a result of the outlet pass from No. 1, he dribbles hard up the side of the court, with the expectation of passing off to the player in the center lane as soon as No. 1 who has taken the middle lane reaches midcourt. As soon as possible, after No. 3 is sure that possession of the ball has been obtained, No. 3 starts upcourt; and as No. 1 takes the middle lane, No. 3 immediately takes the outside lane thereby quickly filling all three lanes. No. 3 may not be able to do this immediately because he cannot leave the vicinity of the basket until he is sure ball possession has been obtained. However, he should be in good position by the time No. 1 is at the free throw area and ready to make the pass off to No. 2 and No. 3. The procedure from this point is the same as in the previous diagrams. Oftentimes in this situation it is possible, because the ball rebounds further outcourt, for No. 1 and No. 2 to collaborate with a two-on-one or a quick break situation and not wait for the pattern to form.

Diagram 9-7 shows a variation of the fast break pattern from the missed shot, with No. 3 obtaining the rebound and making the outlet pass to No. 1 who has moved out to the side of the court. After receiving the pass from No. 3, No. 1 dribbles hard down the side of the court but is unable to continue without veering to the inside because he is being forced to the sideline. In order not to stop the momentum of the fast break, No. 1 immediately drives into the center lane and continues the drive down the center lane until he reaches the free throw circle area. No. 2, after he sees No. 1 take the center lane, cuts behind No. 1 into the outside lane previously occupied by No. 1. No. 4 waits momentarily until he is sure that ball possession has been gained and that No. 3 has been successful in making the outlet pass to No. 1. No. 4 then drives down the outside lane to a position where he can expect a pass off from No. 1 who now has the ball in the free throw circle area. Extreme caution should be exercised here that the players stay spread out and are sure that all three lanes are filled. While it is not possible to get the ball down the floor as quickly as the straight line attack, it sometimes is very effective because, as No. 2 cuts behind No. 1, he is many times overlooked and left unguarded, the defense concentrating on the man with the ball No. 1 and No. 4. Some time will be wasted in the dribble from the outside lane to the inside lane, but it should be remembered that the main objective of this kind of an offense is to outnumber the defense at a time when the offensive team has the ball in good scoring position whether it be a layup type of shot or an unguarded 15 foot outcourt shot.

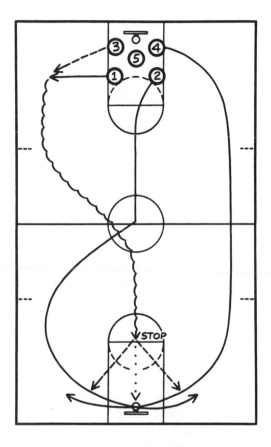

DIAGRAM 9-7

Diagram 9-8 shows the fast break pattern of play after the successful shot. No. 5 gets the rebound and quickly steps out of bounds directly under the basket. He immediately passes to No. 1 who, as soon as the basket is made, moves to the side of the court and readies himself for the pass from No. 5. He should be in approximately the same area as he would be if the ball was passed from No. 5 from a rebounded shot. The pattern of play after No. 1 has received the pass is the same as described in the previous Diagram 9-3. No. 1 moves up the side of the court dribbling fast and hard until he reaches the center line area at which point he passes into No. 2 who has been breaking up the middle lane. In

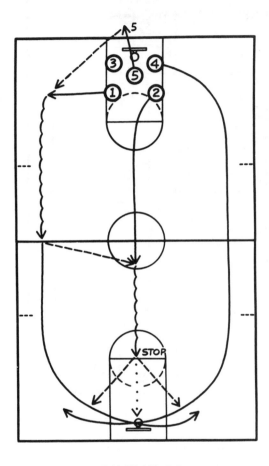

DIAGRAM 9-8

the meantime No. 4, seeing that No. 1 has successfully received the out-
pass from No. 5, breaks down the opposite side of the floor. No. 2 receives
the pass from No. 1 and dribbles to the free throw line area, at which
point he can either pass off to No. 1 or No. 4, or shoot. It should be
repeated here that No. 2 should not receive the ball until he has reached
or is beyond the center circle. One of the strong features of this type of
fast break is that the player in the outside lane is able to advance the ball
rapidly using the dribble because of the fact that there is no congestion
in this area and, as a result, he is able to get the ball to the center area with

little opposition from the opponents until he is ready to pass the ball to the player in the middle lane.

Diagram 9-9 shows the fast break pattern from a missed free throw. No. 1 receives the rebound and immediately makes the outlet pass to No. 4 who has positioned himself near the sidelines as indicated in the diagram. Usually he will not be guarded while in this position. No. 1 should be able to make the outlet pass very quickly from this position and can do so by making a right hand jump pass or a short dribble to clear himself from any congestion he might encounter under the basket making it difficult to clear the ball to No. 4. After No. 4 has received the ball, he

DIAGRAM 9-9

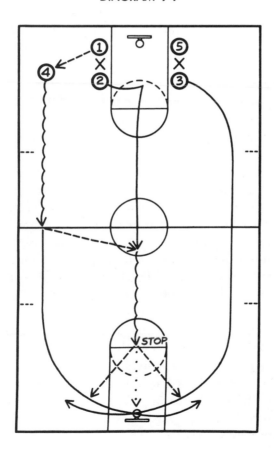

dribbles hard down the side of the floor until such time as he reaches the area where he will make the pass into the middle lane. No. 2 will step in front of the free throw shooter to cut off the rebound should the ball hit the front of the rim. After No. 2 sees that No. 1 has obtained the rebound and has made the outlet pass to No. 4, he immediately cuts up the middle lane. No. 3 cuts up the opposite side of the floor to fill the third lane. It is important that No. 2 and No. 3 remain in their respective positions long enough to help rebound. No. 3 may also step in front of the free thrower to cut off the rebound. No. 2 especially should be careful not to leave too soon because even though the outlet pass is executed quickly it will take some time before No. 4 can receive the ball and get his drive started. This will leave plenty of time for No. 2 to pivot and make his cut up the middle lane.

After No. 4 reaches the passing area he passes the ball into No. 2 who dribbles to the free throw circle area and decides what he should do dependant upon the defensive players position as well as the offensive players position.

Diagram 9-10 shows the fast break pattern after a missed free throw, with the rebound going to No. 2 who has cut off the free thrower from the rebound by stepping in front of him as soon as he is able to do so legally. No. 2, after gaining possession of the ball, makes the outlet pass to No. 4 who has positioned himself in the area shown in the diagram. It should be mentioned here that No. 4 does not remain stationary, but is free to move about as long as he stays in the immediate area and is ready to receive the outlet pass when the passer is ready to make it. He should be careful not to be responsible for any delay as far as the outlet pass is concerned and should make it easy for the passer to make the pass.

After No. 2 has possession of the ball, he turns to his right or left, depending upon the position of his opponents, and makes the outlet pass to No. 4. After No. 4 receives the pass, he drives hard down the side of the court in the outside lane until he reaches the pass-in area. No. 3, after he is sure that No. 2 has possession of the ball and has been successful in making the outlet pass to No. 4, cuts down the middle lane and receives the pass from No. 4 as indicated in the diagram. Meanwhile No. 1, who has been stationed under the basket, after making sure No. 4 has possession of the ball, breaks to the outside of the floor and down the outside lane. No. 3, after having received the pass from No. 4, dribbles to the free throw area where he has the alternative of driving all the way in for the layup, if conditions warrant this maneuver, shooting if he is free

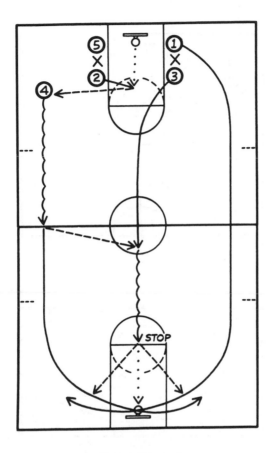

DIAGRAM ·9-10

to do so from the free throw area, or passing off to No. 4 or No. 1 whichever is free to receive a pass. The success of this maneuver will be dependant upon the ability of No. 2 to make the outlet pass to No. 4.

Diagram 9-11 shows a variation of the fast break pattern after a missed free throw. No. 1 obtains the rebound and, being unable to make the direct outlet pass, dribbles toward the sideline and endline a short distance to get out of the congested area or away from the possibility of a held ball situation. After having cleared himself and making it possible to make the pass, he passes to No. 4 who has stationed himself at the side of the court and in a position to receive it. No. 4 cuts up the side of the

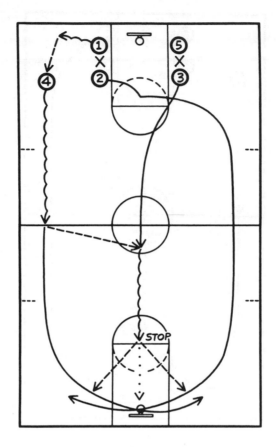

DIAGRAM 9-11

floor in a driving dribble until he reaches the prescribed passing area. No. 2, who steps in front of the free thrower to cut off the possibility of a rebound to him, makes sure the outlet pass has been made to No. 4, cuts up the left side of the floor in the outside lane. No. 3, meanwhile making sure that No. 4 has obtained possession of the ball, moves into the center lane and drives toward the offensive basket. Upon reaching the center circle, he receives the pass from No. 4 and dribbles to the free throw area where he executes one of the several options he has as follows: drive in for the layup, shoot from the free throw area, pass off to either No. 4 or No. 2, or wait for the trailers.

The fact that No. 1 has wasted time in making the outlet pass to

No. 4 will tend to jeopardize the chances of the fast break's success in this particular instance; however it should be remembered that the purpose of the three lane attack is not to beat the defense to the basket with a solo layup, but rather to outnumber the defense with a 2-on-1 or 3-on-2 situation so that the good shot may be obtained. It is also possible that, because of the delay in getting the ball to No. 4, that he will need to maneuver so that he will be in a position to receive the pass from No. 1. This may especially be true if the defensive team is using a full court press. If this is true, No. 4 should move downcourt a short distance and break back to receive the pass. This might also mean that, should No. 4 be unable to dribble the ball up the side of the court, No. 3 (instead of taking the middle lane) will cut over and take the outside lane. No. 4 will pass immediately to No. 3 and No. 2 will take the middle lane. No. 3 will then dribble down the sideline and pass to No. 2. No. 5 will take the other outside lane.

Diagram 9-12 shows the fast break pattern after a free throw is made. The player position is the same as Diagram 9-9 which shows the pattern of play after the missed free throw. Player No. 4 takes the position as indicated in the diagram, with the intention of receiving the pass out from one of the rebounders. This is true in previous Diagrams 9-9 and 9-10. If No. 4 should take a position on the other side of the floor the pattern would be reversed. No. 5 takes the ball after the successful free throw and steps quickly out of bounds. No. 5 cannot make the pass out to No. 4. No. 3 notices that the pass out cannot be made so he immediately moves to the side of the court as indicated in the diagram. No. 5 passes the ball to No. 3 who in turn dribbles quickly up the side of the court until he reaches the middle of the court area. No. 2 steps in front of the free thrower to cut off the rebound possibility, hesitates and when he sees that No. 3 receives the pass he immediately breaks down the center of the court in the center lane. When No. 4 sees the pass go to No. 3 he breaks down the outside lane. This type of play does not necessarily need to be predetermined. When the three lane fast break pattern is employed, and the players practice filling the lanes they automatically fill the lane that is closest to them. There may be a slight mix-up in assignments as the break starts but by the time the players reach center court the adjustments are made and the three lanes are filled. When No. 3 reaches the passing area he makes the pass into No. 2 who in turn dribbles to the free throw area and decides upon the next course of action.

Usually No. 5 takes the ball out of bounds on all successful free

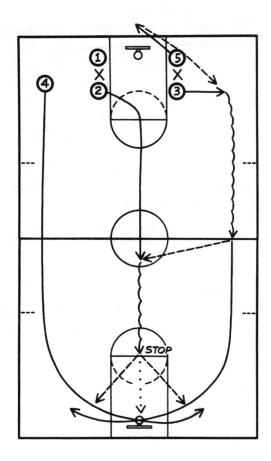

DIAGRAM 9-12

throws and baskets because, as has been mentioned previously, he does most of the rebounding and is always the trailer. A good share of responsibility for the success of the fast break once it reaches center court rests on the shoulders of the middle man. He is more or less the quarterback and usually makes the final decision as to what course of action should be followed once he has the ball.

Diagram 9-13 shows the fast break from the center jump. Although this type of play may be categorized as a special play for a special situation and can be thought of as a quick break play, it still should be included in the repertoire of plays used by a fast break team. This diagram shows

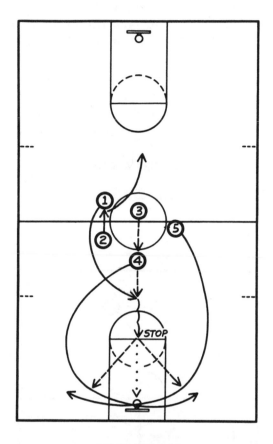

DIAGRAM 9-13

the general placement of players at the center circle and one variation of the pattern which might be used. It should always be remembered that the fast break team is one that is always anxious to run and this attitude will be carried over into all types of situations including jump balls. Diagram 9-13 shows a play that may be used for a quick basket. It will fit into the general pattern which emphasizes the three lane fast break, and yet will not be a dangerous play should possession of the ball not be gained. No. 3 tips the ball directly ahead to No. 4 who in turn flips the ball to No. 1. No. 1 cuts to the basket and to the outside of No. 2 after he has had a screen from him. No. 2 drops back to guard the defensive basket immediately after he has screened for No. 1, in case the tip to No. 4

is not successful and the opposition gains possession of the ball. Even though the center has been controlling the tip only half of the time, possession may mean a quick basket without too much risk.

No. 5, as soon as he sees No. 4 receive the ball and pass to No. 1, cuts down the outside lane. No. 4 can take the outside lane where he can take a pass from No. 1 should No. 1 not be able to go all the way in for the basket.

Diagram 9-14 shows the fast break pattern from the interception or loose ball situation. Here again, as the players break down the floor on the fast break or the quick break, an attempt is made to fill all three lanes

DIAGRAM 9-14

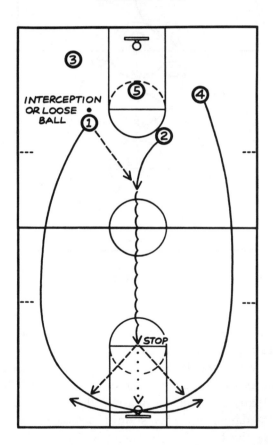

so that each player will know where he can pass the ball when it comes time to pass it. While the interception of a pass or picking up of a loose ball will be more conducive to the use of the quick break (which quite often will either make it possible for a long pass downcourt and an easy lay up or a collaboration of two players against it) it still is good practice to attempt to fill the three lanes so there is no confusion as the players move the ball downcourt.

It should be borne in mind that the positions as shown in the diagram will not be the same but are placed here to illustrate how the lanes can be filled quickly and easily. The players should size up the situation quickly and without hesitation so that the play can materialize before the defense can be formed.

Diagram 9-14 shows No. 1 intercepting the ball. He immediately looks upcourt and passes to No. 2 who cuts up the middle lane. No. 1 drives down the outside lane after making the pass to No. 2 and No. 4 takes the other outside lanes which are shown in the diagram. Usually, in a situation such as this where there is an interception or possession is gained by picking up a loose ball, the player is able to drive all the way to the basket by himself without any help from a teammate; however by filling the lanes the players can get to the basket quickly and be in a position for the rebound if the basket is missed or if the player needs to pass off in case he cannot drive all the way for the layup.

If the defense forms quickly and No. 2 cannot drive in, he stops at the free throw lane as in the regular fast break pattern and follows the same maneuvers—either shooting or waiting until No. 1 and No. 4 are in a position to receive the pass as they are cutting in toward the basket.

10

The Zone Offense

The word *zone* has struck fear into the heart of many a basketball coach. It has caused frustration and destroyed the poise and self confidence of many high scoring basketball teams. It has been legislated against, talked about, and been responsible for the passage of rules which have changed the game itself. There are those who claim that it reduces the game of basketball to nothing more than a shooting contest and that it is ruining basketball. Despite all this, the zone is still very much a part of present-day basketball just as it has been from almost the very beginning of the game.

THE ZONE DEFENSE

The zone defense has stood the test of time and, although there have been many changes and innovations in its use from the stationary zones of yesteryear to the many versions that exist today (including the sliding zone and the zone press), it seems destined to stay. The zone defense has enjoyed periods of popularity and periods of disuse depending largely upon the success of the teams using it and although many coaches dislike it, they must prepare their teams to meet the zone in its many forms.

The zone was introduced about 1914 and it is easy to understand why it became popular. The small floors, low ceilings, the two-handed set shot, and general style of play at that time all contributed to the success of the zone and the reasons for using it. Later on rules changes such as legislation against stalling tactics, the ten-second rule, the three-second rule, the blocking and screen rule all helped to popularize the zone defense.

Many coaches have contributed to the development of the zone defense and its many changes over the years. Among those who were instrumental in its development and used it with great success were Cam Henderson at Davis & Elkins College of West Virginia and later at Marshall College of West Virginia and John Lawther of Pennsylvania State. Both these men were outstanding authorities and strong advocates as well as pioneers in the development of the zone defense.

The zone is still a popular defense even today, but only because it has improved along with the offensive maneuvers and has kept pace with recent innovations in basketball.

However, the change in offensive tactics and improvement in the ability of the players to hit from outcourt using the one-hand jump shot has decreased its effectiveness against the better teams.

Kinds of Zones

There are many types or kinds of zone defenses and combinations of zone defenses just as there are many types of offenses to use against them. Among the most common or orthodox zones are: 1-3-1, 1-2-2, 2-3, 3-2, 2-1-2.

Some others are the full-court or half-court zone press, sagging man-to-man defense, with the tall post man and weak side man zoning the basket, various man-to-man and zone combinations, such as the outcourt men playing man-to-man and the others playing a zone around the basket and alternating the zone defense using several kinds during a single game.

By simply learning slight variations in shifts, the players may well use three or four zones during the same game. Teams are coached to move into different zones automatically, making it very difficult and frustrating to play against with any predetermined form of attack. There are weaknesses in all zones and, of course, the purpose of the offense is to try and exploit these weaknesses. The more common forms of the zone are shown in the following diagrams. The weaknesses of each are shown by the shaded areas.

Diagram 10-1 shows the weaknesses of the 1-3-1 zone. It can readily be seen that the weak areas are on each side of the basket along the baseline. If the offense can get the ball to the deep man along either side of the free throw area, a good shot will be obtained. The 1-3-1 zone attempts to keep three men between the ball and the basket. The three-in-line principle is applied whenever possible so that, if the offensive player gets by the front line of defense, he will immediately encounter a second defensive player. This zone is especially strong in the free throw area and the sides, but decidedly weak in the corners and against the long shot. Special offenses against this 1-3-1 zone would include the 1-3-1, 2-1-2 and 2-2-1. It should be remembered in attacking the 1-3-1 zone that the defense always has one or more players in front of the ball and that the 1-3-1 principle is always in existence no matter where the ball is on the court. The strong areas in this defense are through the middle and on either side of the free throw line area.

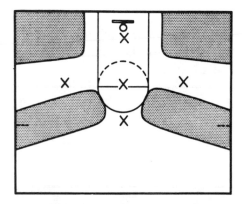

DIAGRAM 10-1

Diagram 10-2 shows the weak areas in the 1-2-2 zone as being through the middle and along the sides. It would be logical, therefore, to place an offensive player in the high post position and in the corners to take advantage of these areas of weakness. It should be remembered, however, that the middle shaded area will not be left open for any length of time. The free throw area is the most vulnerable spot. The attack should be directed to this area, especially during the starting position since the defense will be well spread out during this time, and as the ball is moved, these weak areas disappear. This type of zone is weak against blocking and cutting. It is also weak against rebounding because only two players are

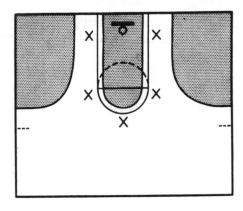

DIAGRAM 10-2

in good rebound position. If a special offense were to be used against this defense, probably the 2-1-2 with the high post and the 1-3-1 would be most acceptable and be most successful.

Diagram 10-3 shows the areas of weakness in the 2-3 zone defense. It can be readily seen that the area through the middle of the defense is

DIAGRAM 10-3

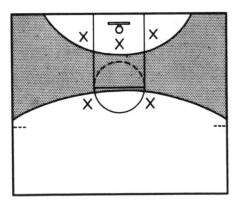

particularly vulnerable. This includes the free throw lane area and the areas on both sides of the free throw line. The areas opposite the free throw line offer excellent opportunities for good shots all the way to the sidelines. The strength of the 2-3 zone lies in the fact that it is extremely strong in rebounding because of the position of the three back men, who in many cases are able to form a triangle around the basket and thereby screen out the offensive rebounders. It is virtually impossible to obtain many offensive rebound baskets against this defense and this feature is the number one objective of the defense. This attribute makes it an ideal defense to use along with the fast break because the two front men do very little rebounding, do much of the outfront defense, and are able to start downcourt as soon as a shot is taken because of the rebound position of the three backcourt players. The best offense against the 2-3 zone is the 1-3-1 because it places players in the areas where the zone is the weakest. The 3-1-1 and 1-2-2 will also be effective. All three offenses spread the defense and place offensive players in the weak areas of the defense.

Diagram 10-4 shows the weak areas in the 3-2 zone as being the free throw area, the corners, and underneath the basket. Good shots should be obtained from these areas. The 3-2 is a very fluid type zone since the players shift into areas previously occupied by a teammate in the process of following the ball. The three front men do a great deal of shifting of

DIAGRAM 10-4

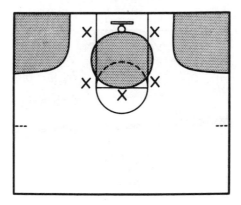

positions, and the responsibility of guarding definite areas is not so much in evidence in the 3-2 zone as in the other types of zone. The territory to be guarded by each player is dictated by the movement and position of the ball at all times.

The 3-2 zone favors the quick break offense because of the excellent position of the front man, which is conducive to this type of maneuver. The weak areas in the 3-2 zone favor the following offensive formations: 2-3, 1-3-1, and 2-2-1. These formations will place men in the areas of known weakness should a special type of zone be used instead of using one offense for all types of zone defenses.

Diagram 10-5 shows the areas of weakness in the 2-1-2 zone. The player alignment indicates that this type of zone will be strong in the middle or against the pivot type of offense. It will be exceedingly strong in rebounding since a triangle can be formed around the basket to screen out offensive rebounders. It is difficult to obtain close-in shots against this type of zone and most of the shooting will need to be done from the outside although it is possible to obtain a few under-the-basket sleepers. It is designed primarily to stop the inside shooting and prevent the ball from being moved into the pivot. Although the free throw area is closed, shots may be obtained from the corners and the sides of the court, as indicated in the diagram. The area directly under the basket is especially vulnerable. The best offensive formations against this type of zone are: 2-3, 1-3-1 and the 3-1-1.

DIAGRAM 10-5

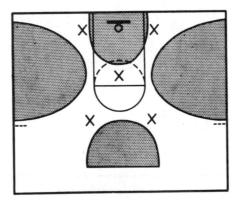

BASIC PRINCIPLES USED IN ATTACKING THE ZONE

The basic principle of the zone defense is that the defensive players play the ball, and their movements depend upon the flight of the ball and the movements of the offense players who are stationed in areas which the defensive players are assigned to guard.

It should be remembered when attacking any zone that certain principles must be considered. Any zone defense presents weaknesses because, when the players shift to strengthen one position, another position or area on the floor is weakened. Therefore, it should be the prime objective of the offensive team to first of all discover this weakness and exploit it. This opportunity is enhanced by having the right kind of offensive players, but even without them the job can be done. Although this theory is sound, it must be determined *first* of all if the zone is being used; *second,* what kind of zone it is; and *third,* whether several types are being used. The easiest method of determining whether the zone is being used is by sending a player through the middle and out again. If he is not picked up, then it is reasonably certain that some type of zone is being used.

Another problem encountered in attacking the zone is that many teams will switch zones or switch from the zone to the man-to-man style of play, thereby confusing the offense. This is done by switching from a man-to-man to a zone after a score is made. Different zones are used depending upon whether the score is odd or even, such as the 1-3-1 and 1-2-2 and the 3-2 zone when the score is odd, and the 2-1-2 and 2-3 when the score is even.

The main purpose of the zone as used by many coaches is to catch the other team "off" in their outcourt shooting on a particular night. By using several types of zones and changing them continually, it will tend to confuse the offense and make it difficult to set up an offensive pattern.

THEORIES USED IN BEATING THE ZONE

There are offenses designed to beat the zone no matter what kind of a zone it is. Basically there are four theories, one or all of which may be used in beating the zone defense: (1) *overloading,* whereby there are more offensive players placed in an area than there are defensive players to cover them; (2) *passing the ball* so quickly, with short, fast passing, that the defense cannot keep up with the ball until it is too late and a good percentage shot is obtained; (3) *moving the players* in a predetermined pattern in such a way that the defense cannot cope with guarding both players and areas; (4) *screening the defensive players* out of the play so that a high-percentage shot may be obtained from a predetermined position on the floor.

Overloading

The overload principle has been one way of attacking the zone for many years and many coaches firmly believe it is the best method of obtaining the good shots. Overloading is simply placing more offensive players in an area than there are defensive players to guard them. The players can be moved from one side of the court to the other, thereby creating a complicated situation for the defense because the defensive player who is assigned to cover a particular area or a specific amount of floor space, finds two players in the area making it impossible for him to cover them both. By placing two or more offensive players in a particular area that is to be guarded by a defensive player, it means that other defensive players are guarding an area in which there are no offensive players.

The Set Principle

The set principle is probably the oldest form of attacking the zone. It places a premium on good shooting and this could be one of its glaring weaknesses. Basically the idea is sound because it is impossible for players to move fast enough to cover the areas designated for them to cover if the ball is passed quickly and accurately. In this offense, definite passing lanes are established and the players move only a step or two in one direction or another so that their teammates know the position they will be in when it is time for them to receive a pass. This pattern demands excellent ballhandling, passing, and patience, but it does result in good shots and excellent opportunities for good shots. The idea is to move the ball faster than the defense can shift. Moving the ball in perfect unison, using good teamwork and cooperation among the players, along with a predetermined method or pattern of attack, will beat the zone. Against the man-to-man style of play, one or two players may work together to set up a shot but, against the zone, it takes all five players working as a closely knit unit. Sloppy passing, poor ballhandling, and lack of cooperation will allow any zone defense to shut off the offense completely.

Player Movement

Another method of beating the zone is by movement of the players or cutting through the zone. While it is true that the player cannot dribble through the zone, it is possible for the player to move freely through the zone without the ball in his possession, and to do so using a continuity of play that will leave him in certain designated areas which will be similar in nature to the overload principle or set pattern. In using the cutter type of attack, the player is a passer, cutter, screener, or shooter, in that order. The purpose of this method is to place offensive players in areas that are not covered by the defensive players often enough so that one will free himself for a shot. It often results in two players being in the same area that is being guarded by one defensive player. These cutting patterns are so designed as to place the offensive player either in the free, open area or in the area between the defensive players who have not had time to shift to the assigned area. The idea is to get the defense to become careless, overshift or undershift, leaving an open area.

In the player movement, the players should always come to meet the ball. The players should cut between the guarded areas at a time when the zone is shifting. The use of head and body feints and faking should be a part of the passing technique and will do much to disturb the defense.

Screening

The use of screens is more or less a recent innovation in attacking the zone. The idea of the screen is to cut off a player away from the ball or prevent him from getting to the floor area he is supposed to cover in time to prevent the shot. This can be done by moving the ball to one side of the floor or the other and, in the process the screen is set on the defensive player as he moves back to his defensive position. In the meantime an offensive player has moved into the area the defensive man is assigned to cover, and the ball is passed to him for an unguarded shot. The screened-out player is not able to move to this area in time to prevent the shot. This type of screening can take place anywhere on the floor and has proven to be very effective.

BASIC ELEMENTS IN THE ZONE ATTACK

1. Players should not stand around. There must be constant movement in order that the passing lanes will be opened up.

2. Teams use the zone for various reasons and these reasons should be discovered and exploited.
3. Move the ball.
4. Get good rebounding position. Most zone defense teams place their best rebounders in the back court position; consequently, the offensive rebounders must fight for position.
5. Set up good shots.
6. Make the pattern basic so that it is easily understood by all the players and can be used against all zones as well as man-to-man.
7. Screen the zone whenever possible. This can be done more easily near the basket area.
8. Strive for good floor balance. Keep the continuity so that continuous movement of all players can take place.
9. Work behind the backcourt men. This will make the backcourt defense honest and open up the middle area.
10. Place a man in the middle of the zone so that the defense cannot use their defensive players to force out-court shooting. The ball can also be passed into the middle, forcing the defense to sag, allowing the pivot man to pass back out for a better shot.

DECIDING ON THE OFFENSE

There are three decisions to make regarding the offense to be used in the zone attack:

1. *A separate attack for each zone.* This entails a variety of offenses which can be used effectively against every kind or type of zone encountered. As shown in the preceding diagrams every zone has weak spots and the offense should be geared to take advantage of these weak points. This necessitates the learning of a different offense for every zone defense. This requires a great deal of practice and patience; however, it does exploit the weak points in each zone.

2. *An attack to take care of all zones.* By using only one offense, it can be learned well enough and executed well enough that it offsets any advantage which might be gained by attacking the zone at its weakest point by using a variety of offenses. It is better to do one thing well than many things poorly. A single offense to be used against all zones will save a great deal of time and effort. The fact that the players can learn one offense well so that each player knows exactly what is required of him will more than offset the advantage of exploiting the defense at its weakest points by using a separate offense for every zone defense.

3. *A zone attack out of the regular man-for-man alignment to take care of switching defenses.* There are those who believe that the same

attack should be used against both the man-to-man and the zone. They contend that it is better to learn one offense well than several poorly.

By using one offense, the players learn it well and execute it well. They do not become rattled by trying to determine if the other team is playing a certain type of zone or man-to-man or switching from one to the other. They have confidence in the offense they are using and go about their business of using it regardless of the defensive tactics of their opponents. The same principles used in the man-for-man offense may be used against the zone. The players are cutting, picking, and driving against the zone the same as they are against the man-for-man defense.

Difficulty Encountered in Attacking the Zone

One difficulty in playing against the zone and one reason for employing one offense against the zone is that any team that can play a good zone is able to shift from one type to another easily and with good results. This poses a tremendous problem offensively since it means that, every time the defense changes, the offense must also change to match up against the zone. It is far more difficult to learn an offense than it is a defense, and this would mean that a team would need a separate offense for every zone defense, a near impossibility.

The Use of One Offense Against All Defenses

There are many specific patterns which can be used against different defenses, but it stands to reason that the players cannot be expected to have an offense ready for any defense which a team might spring on them. The solution is to employ an offense that will work against all defenses. The moving 1-3-1 offense which can be easily adjusted to any type of defense would seem to be the logical solution.

A good zone offense should be the same as the man-for-man offense. It should entail the following:

1. It must be similar in the basic movements.
2. There must be a man playing behind the defense to make it honest.
3. It must be fluid enough to meet the changing defenses.
4. There should be a man playing on the free throw area.
5. The overload principle must be in evidence.
6. There must be cutting of players constantly.

USE OF THE 1-3-1 AGAINST ALL ZONES

The 1-3-1 offense is probably the most suitable of all the offenses against any type of zone. This offense places heavy pressure on the zone, and the advantages created by the zone are eliminated in many respects. The most important advantage of using the 1-3-1 against the zone is that it also can be used effectively against the man-to-man style of play, so there is no need to change should the defense switch from the zone to the man-to-man style of play and vice versa as so many teams now have the habit of doing.

The 1-3-1 is particularly effective against the 2-1-2 and the 3-2 zone defenses because there is a better chance to split the zone, making it almost impossible to cover all the players. Thus, it is possible to get good inside shots and place greater pressure on the entire zone. Each player should know his position, and the offensive triangle should be maintained at all times. The offensive players should keep well spread out so that one or two men cannot guard them. If they are situated far enough apart, the zone will have gaps through which passes can be made. These gaps will take time to close.

The 1-3-1 offense is able to place players in open areas in all the zones, with the weakest defense probably being the 1-3-1. It has an advantage of always having an offensive player behind the defense at all times. The 1-3-1 offense will produce the good shot against any kind of zone even though the zone is constantly being changed. The basic moves of the 1-3-1 are also equally effective against the man-for-man defense. In any attack against the zone, set plays should not be used to any great extent and the concentration should be on passing the ball and controlled player movement. The ball cannot be moved with quickness and sureness until and unless there is someone to pass it to when it is ready to be passed. Consequently, the pattern of movement of both the player and the ball should be such that there is continuity at all times. Because of the constant threat of changing zone defenses, a systematic way of combating all zones regardless of the type or combination should be used. It is necessary to have a system that can be learned easily and one that will be used effectively against all zones plus the man-to-man style of play.

The 1-3-1 encourages the players to move more freely and interchange offensive positions, which is one of the basic ingredients in beating the zone. Many zone defenses are established to stop the close-in shot and allow the outside shot. Fast and clever movement of the players will not allow this to happen. Movement of the players and the ball is a "must" if the zone is to be defeated. It becomes very difficult for the defense to function against this style of play especially if it is accompanied with good outside shooting. The outside shooting will tend to bring the defense out which will allow the openings for the offensive players to receive passes as they are cutting through the zone.

ADVANTAGES OF THE 1-3-1 ZONE OFFENSE

1. Places men in the weak spots of most zone defenses.
2. Creates a one-on-one situation.
3. Spreads out the defense.
4. Places a rebounder near the basket.
5. Places a man behind the defense.
6. Keeps a man back on defense.
7. Creates good offensive rebounding position.
8. Places a man in the middle.
9. Can be used against a variety of defenses.
10. Gives good defensive balance.
11. Provides good outside shooting.
12. Provides good inside shots.
13. Provides good opportunities for the quick break.
14. Permits players greater freedom in their use of specialized abilities.
15. Tends to create a one-on-one situation

DISADVANTAGES OF THE 1-3-1 ZONE OFFENSE

1. Responsibility is placed on the front player, known as the quarterback.
2. Lacks defensive strength.
3. The personnel requirements are very exacting.
4. Must have good set shots.
5. Must have good pivot player.
6. Must have good ballhandler out front.

PERSONNEL FOR THE 1-3-1 OFFENSE

The players determine the success of any offense and the zone offense, no matter what kind it is, is no exception.

In setting up the 1-3-1 against the zone, it is only natural that the point or front man and the middle man are the most important. The point man will handle the ball a good share of the time, will direct the play, set the tempo of play and be generally thought of as the quarterback. His responsibilities are to direct the attack. He should have certain qualifications which include the following: (1) average height; (2) good passer; (3) possess excellent judgment; (4) a good defensive player as he will have the defensive responsibility if the ball is intercepted; (5) good outshooter; (6) possess poise.

The center man or middle man should be versatile and be quick. He should be able to turn and shoot, drive, and be a good passer and faker.

The side players should be good jump shooters and be able to fake and drive. These players should also be good passers and be able to get the ball into the middleman as most of the passes into the middle usually will be made from the side of the court.

The deep man or back man is usually the biggest and best rebounder, and this is what he is used for mostly. He makes the back defensive players honest for, unless he is guarded, it is possible for the side men to get the ball to him directly under the basket. He should be able to pass off when he is required to do so.

The following series of diagrams will show the 1-3-1 offense patterns against all types of zone defenses. The patterns show a continuity of play obtained by the interchange of positions by the players, using the movement or cutting pattern with options as to when passes are made and shots taken. The patterns show the movements of the players and the ball. It does not show every opportunity there would be to shoot, as this would be entirely dependent upon whether the opportunity for a shot would exist at specific times during the maneuvers. The decision as to whether a shot should be taken would depend upon the judgment of the individual player.

The first six diagrams (Diagrams 10-6 thru 10-11) show a continuity of play whereby the point player and the pivot man play only these positions while the other three players are exchanging positions constantly.

DIAGRAM 10-6

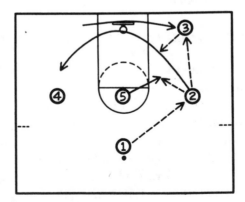

Diagram 10-6 shows No. 1 passing to No. 2 who shoots if he has an open shot. If No. 2 does not shoot he may pass to No. 3 who cuts to the side of the court near the endline when he sees that No. 2 is not going to attempt a shot. He also has the option of passing to No. 5 in the pivot position. No. 2 cuts toward the basket with the expectation of receiving a return pass from No. 3. If the ball is passed quickly before the defense is able to shift, the passing lane may be open and No. 3 may be able to get the ball to No. 2 for a close in shot. If No. 2 or No. 5 does not receive the pass, No. 3 has the option of shooting or passing back to No. 1 who has moved over into a position where he is able to receive the pass. No. 2 cuts under the basket. If No. 3 shoots Nos. 2, 4, and 5 are in excellent rebounding position.

Diagram 10-7 shows the continuity of play if No. 3 chooses not to pass or is unable to pass to No. 5, No. 2, or does not shoot. No. 3 passes back to No. 1 and then takes the position previously occupied by No. 2. No. 4 cuts under the basket and takes the position previously occupied by No. 3. No. 2 now assumes the position occupied by No. 4. No. 1 dribbles toward the center of the court; however he may pass directly back to No. 3 and the play may be run over again because all personnel will be in the correct position and perfect floor balance will exist just as it was when the first pass by No. 1 to No. 2 took place. No. 1 may also pass the

DIAGRAM 10-7

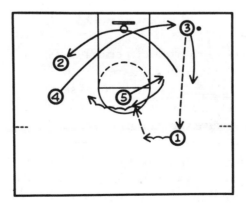

ball into the pivot position depending upon whether or not the passing lane is open as a result of the player movement.

Diagram 10-8 shows No. 1 dribbling to his left as quickly as possible and passing to No. 2, setting up the pattern on the opposite side of the floor. Notice that the 1-3-1 pattern is still maintained. No. 1 also has the option of passing into the pivot should the passing lane be open as a

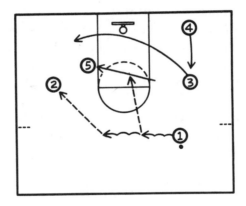

DIAGRAM 10-8

result of the defensive shifting of personnel. No. 4 assumes the position vacated by No. 3. No. 3 cuts underneath the basket to the position formerly occupied by No. 2. As soon as No. 3 sees that No. 2 is not going to shoot he immediately moves over to the side of the court so that he will be in position to receive the pass from No. 2.

Diagram 10-9 shows No. 2 passing to No. 3. No. 2 cuts for the basket immediately after the pass in hopes of finding the passing lane open should the defense fail to shift fast enough to make the adjustment. No. 3 has five options. He may pass quickly to No. 2 if No. 2 is open. He may pass in to No. 5. He may shoot. He may fake a shot and take one dribble around the player who has shifted into the immediate area where he is located or he may pass back out to No. 1. No. 4 assumes the position previously occupied by No. 3 and No. 2 assumes No. 4's previous position.

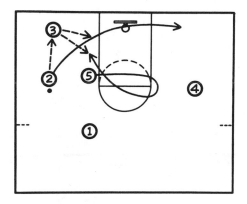

DIAGRAM 10-9

The 1-3-1 formation is still maintained and the continuity can be continued without rearranging the personnel.

Diagram 10-10 shows No. 3 passing the ball to No. 1. The pass back to No. 1 is made if No. 3 is not able to initiate the moves described in

DIAGRAM 10-10

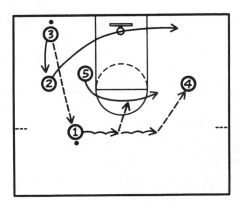

the previous diagram. After the pass to No. 1 No. 3 moves up and takes
the position previously occupied by No. 2. No. 1 dribbles quickly toward
the middle of the court. He may pass in to No. 5 who is moving across
the free throw area or to No. 4.

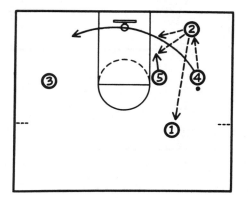

DIAGRAM 10-11

Diagram 10-11 shows the ball being passed from No. 4 to No. 2 who
moved to the side of the court so as to receive the pass. Here again No. 4
has the option of passing to No. 5, 2 or shooting. No. 2 upon receiving
the pass may shoot or pass to No. 4 who cuts immediately upon making
the pass to No. 2. No. 2 may give No. 4 a return pass if the passing lane
is open and No. 4 is in a position to receive the pass. No. 2 may also pass
to No. 5 or pass back out to No. 1.

The following pattern also shows the continuity of play from 1-3-1
offense but involves all five players interchanging positions. There are
many options from this pattern but only the basic maneuvers will be
shown.

Diagram 10-12 shows No. 1 passing the ball to No. 2 who has the
option of shooting if he is open. The distance No. 2 is positioned from

the free throw circle area and the side line will depend to a large degree upon the kind of zone the defense is playing. If the defense is playing a 1-3-1 zone this will mean that No. 2 will play wider because the defense will force him to play wide. As soon as No. 3 sees that No. 2 has or will receive the pass from No. 2 he moves to the position shown in the dia-

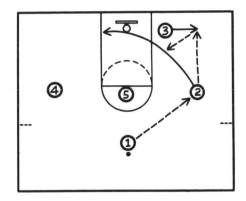

DIAGRAM 10-12

gram. If No. 2 decides not to shoot or is unable to do so he passes to No. 3 who has positioned himself for the pass. If No. 3 is not open No. 2 can pass back to No. 1 and the ball can be taken to the other side of the floor. If the passing has been quick No. 3 may have an opportunity for a good shot. If not he may pass to No. 2 who cuts for the basket as soon as he makes the pass to No. 3. If he cuts immediately the passing lane may be open for the return pass.

Diagram 10-13 shows No. 3 with the ball. He has continued the continuity of play in as much as he has been unable to shoot or pass to No. 2 as suggested in the previous diagram. As soon as No. 2 cuts and No. 5 sees that he is not going to receive the pass he moves down the lane behind No. 2 with the expectation of receiving a pass from No. 3. No. 2 continues his movement underneath the basket and across the free throw lane and takes the side position originally occupied by No. 4. No. 1 will now move

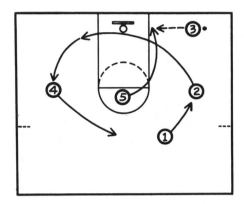

DIAGRAM 10-13

to the side position previously occupied by No. 2. The 1-3-1 formation is intact and the continuity of play may continue should it be necessary to do so and none of the passing lanes were open as a result of the player movements or no shot was taken.

DIAGRAM 10-14

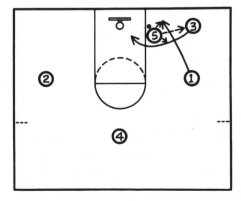

Diagram 10-14 shows the continuity of the pattern if the ball is passed to No. 5 and he does not have an opportunity to shoot. No. 5 can make a return pass to No. 3 if No. 3 does not make his cut but decides to hold his position. No. 5 also has the option of passing to No. 1. No. 3 can also split off No. 5 and cut for a possible return pass and jump shot. Should No. 3 not return the pass from No. 5, No. 4 moves out to the point or position previously occupied by No. 1. No. 2 takes No. 4's former position.

Diagram 10-15 shows a variation of the previous play if No. 1 remains stationary and No. 5 did not receive the pass from No. 3. No. 3 now passes the ball back to No. 1 and cuts for the basket for a return pass from No. 1. No. 1 has the option of shooting if he is open. He may also pass back out to No. 4 who has assumed the point or outside position. If No. 5 does not receive the pass from No. 3 he continues his movement across the lane and returns to the high post position. The players are now in the starting position of the 1-3-1 offense.

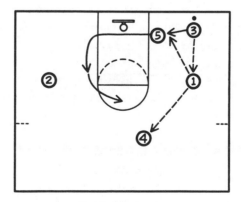

DIAGRAM 10-15

Diagram 10-16 shows the continuity of play if No. 1 does not pass to No. 3 but instead passes to No. 4. No. 4 passes to No. 2 and the pattern now can continue on the opposite side of the floor. No. 2 passes to No. 3

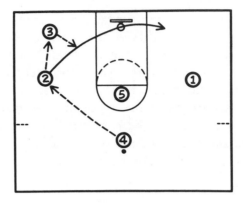

DIAGRAM 10-16

who has moved to the corner so that the pattern may be continued. No. 2 cuts quickly and the procedure is the same as it was on the opposite side of the floor.

The following diagrams describe the 1-3-1 pattern with a continuity of play which is similar in some respects to the two previous patterns described yet moves the players into different passing lanes and cutting paths. These three patterns can be easily learned and will provide enough variation of player movement so that the defense cannot determine what patterns are being used.

The options presented in this pattern will provide opportunities for open shots from the weak areas in the different types or kinds of zones which might be used. The middle area, the areas on either side of the basket and close in, the wide areas and the area out front are all vulnerable at one time or another during the continuity of play using the pattern presented.

Diagram 10-17 shows the ball being passed to No. 4. No. 4 has the option of shooting if he has a good shot or passing to No. 3 who is stationed near the end line and between the free throw lane and the sidelines. If No. 4 does not shoot and passes to No. 3 he cuts across the lane as shown in the diagram to the other side of the court. No. 3 may shoot

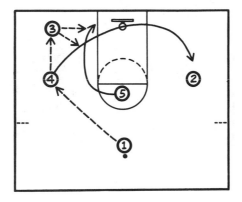

DIAGRAM 10-17

if he has a good shot or pass to No. 4 cutting across the lane or to No. 5 who cuts down from the high post toward the basket.

Diagram 10-18 shows No. 3 passing back to No. 1 who has moved down near the free throw area. No. 3 did not take the option to shoot or pass to No. 4 or No. 5 as mentioned in the description in Diagram 10-17. No. 2 breaks into the free throw lane area at the high post and looks for a pass from No. 1 if No. 1 is not able to obtain a good shot. No. 4 takes the position vacated by No. 2.

Diagram 10-19 shows the position of the players and the continuity of play if No. 1 is not able to shoot or pass into the high post to No. 2 who had broken into this area expecting a pass from No. 1. No. 2 seeing that No. 1 cannot make the pass moves out quickly to the point position previously occupied by No. 1 and receives the pass from No. 1. The ball is moved to the other side of the floor and the continuity of play continues. The ball should be moved quickly but enough time should be allowed so that the passing lanes will be open and advantage can be taken of the inability of the defensive players to cover all areas adequately. This will result in openings within the defense and will provide an opportunity for the offensive players to receive the pass and obtain the desired shot.

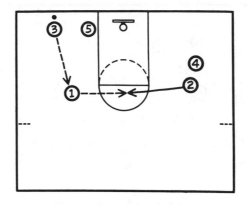

DIAGRAM 10-18

DIAGRAM 10-19

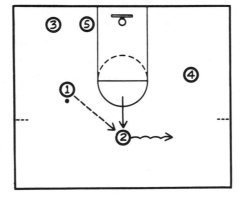

Diagram 10-20 shows No. 2 passing to No. 4. No. 4 has the option of shooting or passing to No. 5 who has moved underneath the basket to a position near the end line and midway between the sideline and free throw lane. No. 5 may shoot or pass to No. 4 who cuts across the free throw lane area toward the basket with the expectation of receiving a return pass from No. 5. No. 5 may also pass to No. 3 who breaks into the free

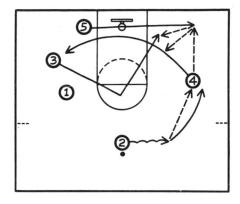

DIAGRAM 10-20

DIAGRAM 10-21

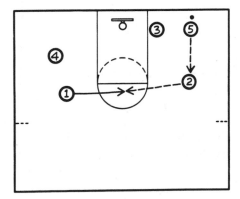

throw area and then down the lane as shown in the diagram. This maneuver will place pressure on the defense under the basket area and in the middle area.

Diagram 10-21 shows the ball being passed back to No. 2 to continue the continuity of play if No. 5 has not executed any of the options pre-

viously mentioned. No. 2 now has the opportunity to shoot or pass into
No. 1 who breaks into the high post area. No. 5's decision not to execute
the options mentioned in the previous diagram should be based on his
judgment as to whether the passing lanes were open and the opportunity
which existed for the receivers of his pass to obtain a good shot. These
opportunities will depend to a great extent upon the zone defense that is
being played.

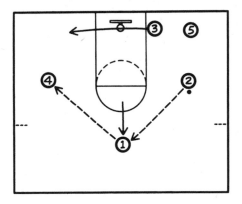

DIAGRAM 10-22

Diagram 10-22 shows No. 2 passing to No. 1 who has moved out
quickly to the point position when he sees that No. 2 is not able to pass
the ball to him in the post position. No. 1 now may shoot or pass to No. 4.
No. 3 moves underneath the basket to the other side of the free throw
lane and readies himself for the pass which may come from No. 4 if
No. 4 does not shoot. The continuity of play will then be continued
until such time as a shot is attempted.

Index